CW01394847

Doggy
POSITIVITY

Doggy

POSITIVITY

Life Lessons from the Ugly Pug who became a Star

Peggy the Hairless Pug

HarperNorth

HarperNorth
Windmill Green
24 Mount Street
Manchester M2 3NX

A division of
HarperCollins*Publishers*
1 London Bridge Street
London SE1 9GF

www.harpercollins.co.uk

HarperCollins*Publishers*
Macken House, 39/40 Mayor Street Upper
Dublin 1, D01 C9W8, Ireland

First published by HarperCollins*Publishers* 2025

1 3 5 7 9 10 8 6 4 2

© P M Entertainment 2025
All photographs (C) Holly Middleton

Peggy the Pug asserts the moral right to
be identified as the author of this work

A catalogue record of this book is
available from the British Library

HB ISBN 978-0-00-877490-5

Printed and bound in the UK using 100%
renewable electricity at CPI Group (UK) Ltd

All rights reserved. No part of this publication may be
reproduced, stored in a retrieval system, or transmitted,
in any form or by any means, electronic, mechanical,
photocopying, recording or otherwise, without the
prior written permission of the publishers.

Without limiting the exclusive rights of any author, contributor or the publisher of
this publication, any unauthorised use of this publication to train generative
artificial intelligence (AI) technologies is expressly prohibited. HarperCollins also
exercise their rights under Article 4(3) of the Digital Single Market Directive 2019/790
and expressly reserve this publication from the text and data mining exception.

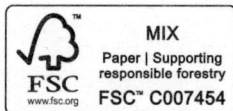

MIX
Paper | Supporting
responsible forestry
FSC
www.fsc.org
FSC™ C007454

This book contains FSC™ certified paper and other controlled
sources to ensure responsible forest management.

For more information visit: www.harpercollins.co.uk/green

To Max and Zak - the best big brothers a dog could have

Contents

Introduction:
Paws for thought

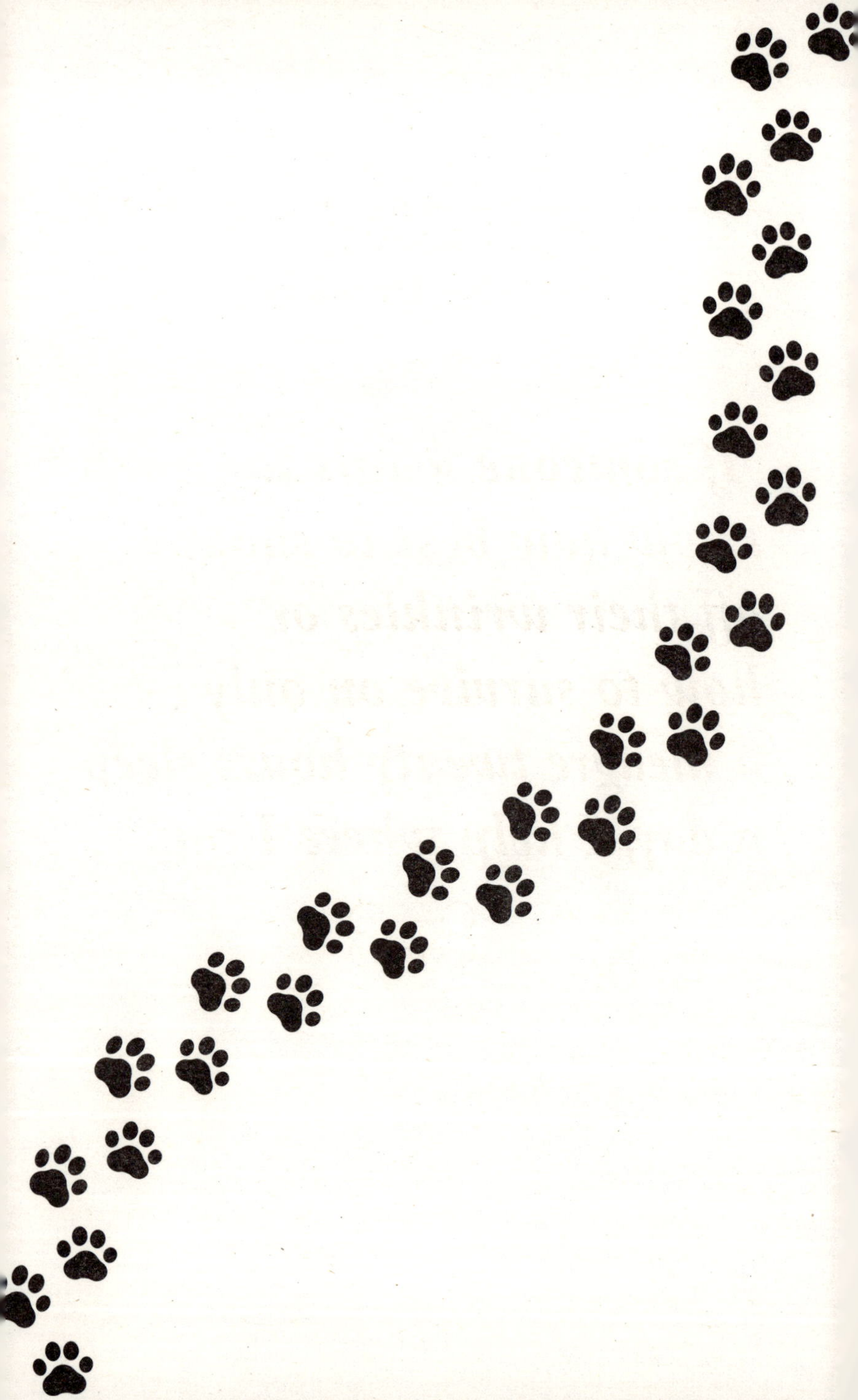

'If someone wants to know how best to show off their wrinkles or how to survive on only a meagre twenty hours sleep a day, I help where I can.'

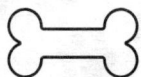

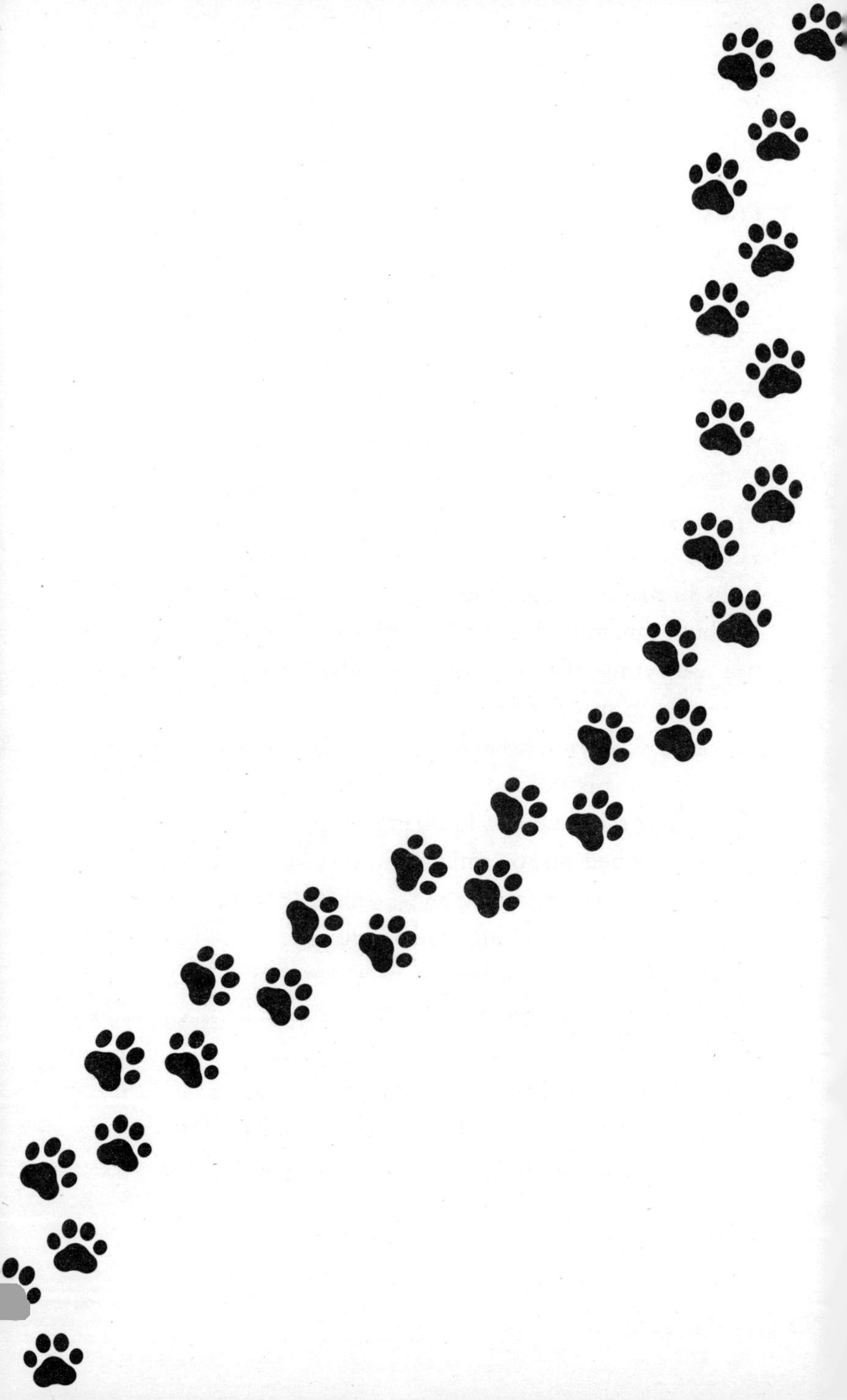

I get it – life can be tough. Look at me, a stunning example of dogkind and yet (hard to believe, I know) some people think I'm ugly. But from Hull to Hollywood, I've never let other people's issues hold me back. And along the way, some of the friends I've met (four-footed or two-legged) have asked me for advice. But writing it down had always been a pipe-dream (typing isn't one of my core skills, I'll admit). But then I got the gig as Dogpool, in *Deadpool & Wolverine*. Even though I thought *Dogpool* would have been a snappier name for the film, I put my editorial notes aside and threw myself into life with my co-stars. I remember being immediately drawn to Ryan Reynolds because of the intense sweetness of his scent. It transpires that Ryan takes daily baths in maple syrup, believing it gives Canadians superpowers. We both ran around in circles with excitement, yelping; it really was a meeting of minds. But, over the next seven months, we were able to successfully train Ryan and the shoot was (eventually) an absolute joy. It taught me a lot about the confusing creature that is mankind, and I like to think that went both ways.

'Peg,' he said one day, lowering his sunglasses and looking at me as I bobbed on my inflatable pizza slice pool float. 'You've always given such great advice,' he smiled. 'You have to write that book you're always talking about writing!'

That afternoon I laughed it off. Ryan is one of life's incorrigible optimists, even down to thinking that I'd be able to distil my experience into a few short pages. So that day I honestly thought nothing of it, just had another couple of sausage martinis and took a car back up the hill to my house. But later that evening, as I carefully chewed my furry unicorn, I began to think seriously about it.

Was it really so outlandish an idea?

After all, hadn't I made my way from a Yorkshire upbringing to the summit of Hollywood? A classic wags-to-riches story. Yes, I'd had advantages that others hadn't — the natural lack of excess hair, the generosity of nipple, tongue, etc. — but I'd also worked hard, damned hard, to get where I was. And I've certainly never believed that true beauty was anywhere other than on the inside. I have always been passionate about lifting up everyone around me. I've never sought to be a guru, but nor am I one to refuse to share my experience when asked — if someone wants to know how best to show off your wrinkles or how to survive on only a meagre twenty hours sleep a day, I help where I can. And along the way I've picked up a lot of tales (non-waggy ones) and collected enough stories for several lifetimes. I realised there were things I needed to say and, more than that, people who might find something in these tips and tricks that will always have you barking up the right tree.

The next day, I sat down and the stories just poured out. I realised that this book wasn't just possible, it was essential. This book has been written as I've travelled back and forth from the quiet East Yorkshire village where I live when I'm not globetrotting. Snatched moments in the breaks between filming, shoots, interviews and signing pawtographs. It's a dog's life.

I will say here, right from the start, that it was the publishers – not me – who put the frankly rather rude subtitle on this book. I'd suggested *Life Lessons from a Fabulous Four-Footed Legend*, which I thought summed it up nicely. Imagine my surprise when they came back with *Life Lessons from the Ugly Pug who became a Star*. Of course, I'd taken my first steps on the hard road to fame with Ugly Pet contests, but really, I know when people are just envious of what I like to call my 'big nip energy'. And as I hope this humble book will show, beauty really is in the eye of the beholder.

I imagine this book will be primarily of interest to humans, although I know many dogs will also find themselves nodding along in recognition. After all, we have much to learn from each other. For example, I have always thought that there was something deeply significant about dogs' and humans' very different reactions towards having an itchy posterior. For a dog, the obvious solution is to make use of the floor and, adjusting their posture accordingly, elegantly drag their rump along the carpet until the itch is no more. Whereas humans, as if keen to deny the existence of a backside at all, go about it secretively, checking to see if anyone is behind them. Only then, like a lone gunman on an arsey knoll, do they venture into the region for a weak scratch. My dear reader, know this, you should never be ashamed of your own butt. I know you humans choose to keep yours covered, as if it's a secret that must be kept, and seem to prefer shaking hands to checking out each other's backsides. For us good dogs, it is both our first and last port of call whenever we greet, or bid farewell to a friend. (And often quite an important part of the middle bit of the meeting as well.) If you take nothing else from this book, I hope it is that you feel liberated to celebrate the magnificent joys of a good butt-scratch.

I hope, too, that the wisdom in this book helps you to keep your tail wagging: live in the moment, find joy in the simple things, love more fully, forgive more easily, embrace curiosity and how to sniff out snacks, as well as communicate better and live a more authentic and fulfilled life. As I always say: 'Eat well, nap often, accept adoration with grace, and never walk if there's a chance someone will carry you.'

This book is all of the advice I wish I'd known before setting off on this madcap journey we call life. Some of it may stretch credulity, but every single word of it is true. Paw on heart.

Love, Peggy

Lesson 1: Find your pack

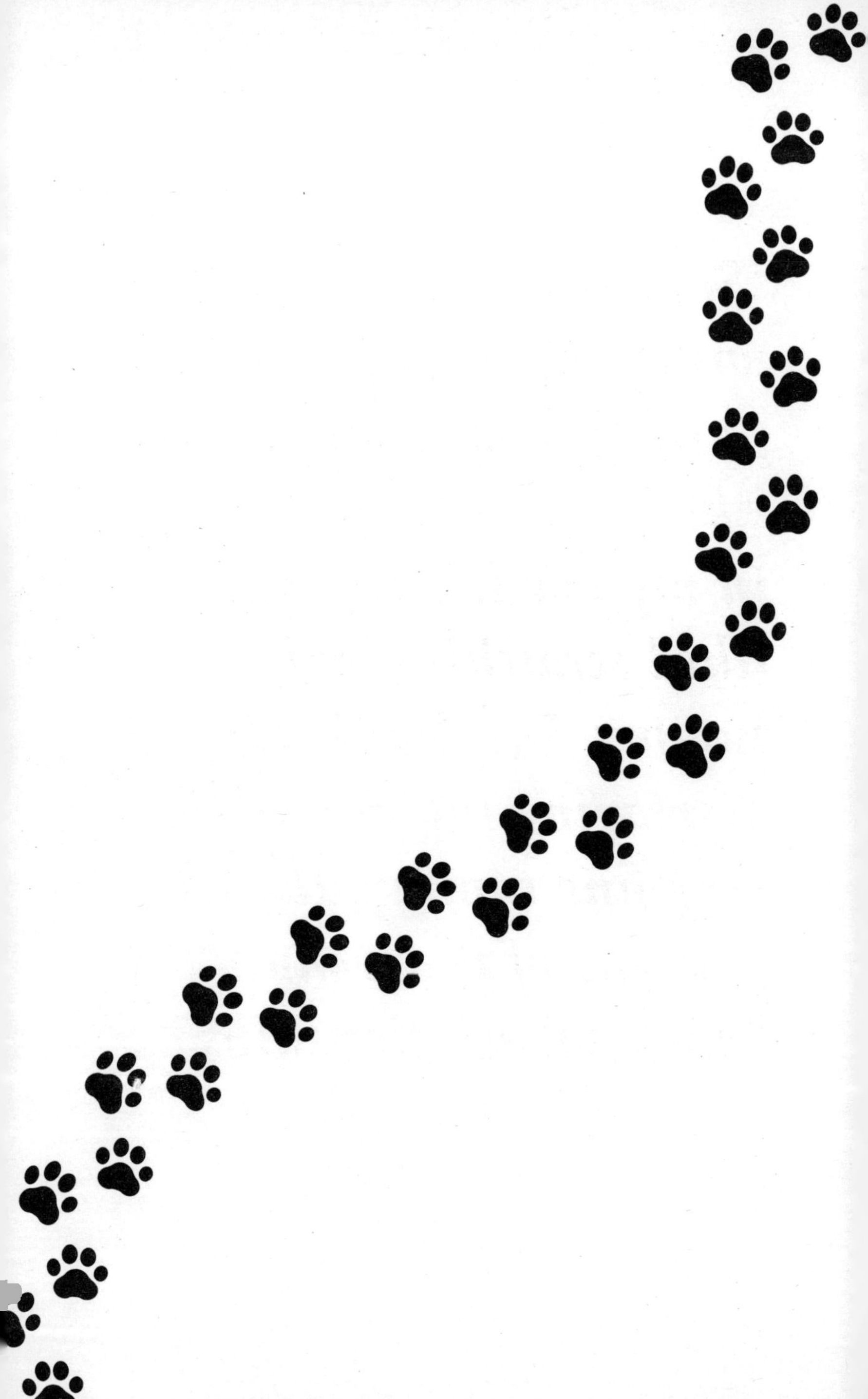

'Sometimes you just click with people. They liked putting food in my bowl. I liked it when they put food in my bowl. They really liked scratching my tummy. I really liked displaying my admittedly very fine tummy. It was just one of those mutually beneficial relationships.'

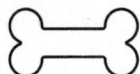

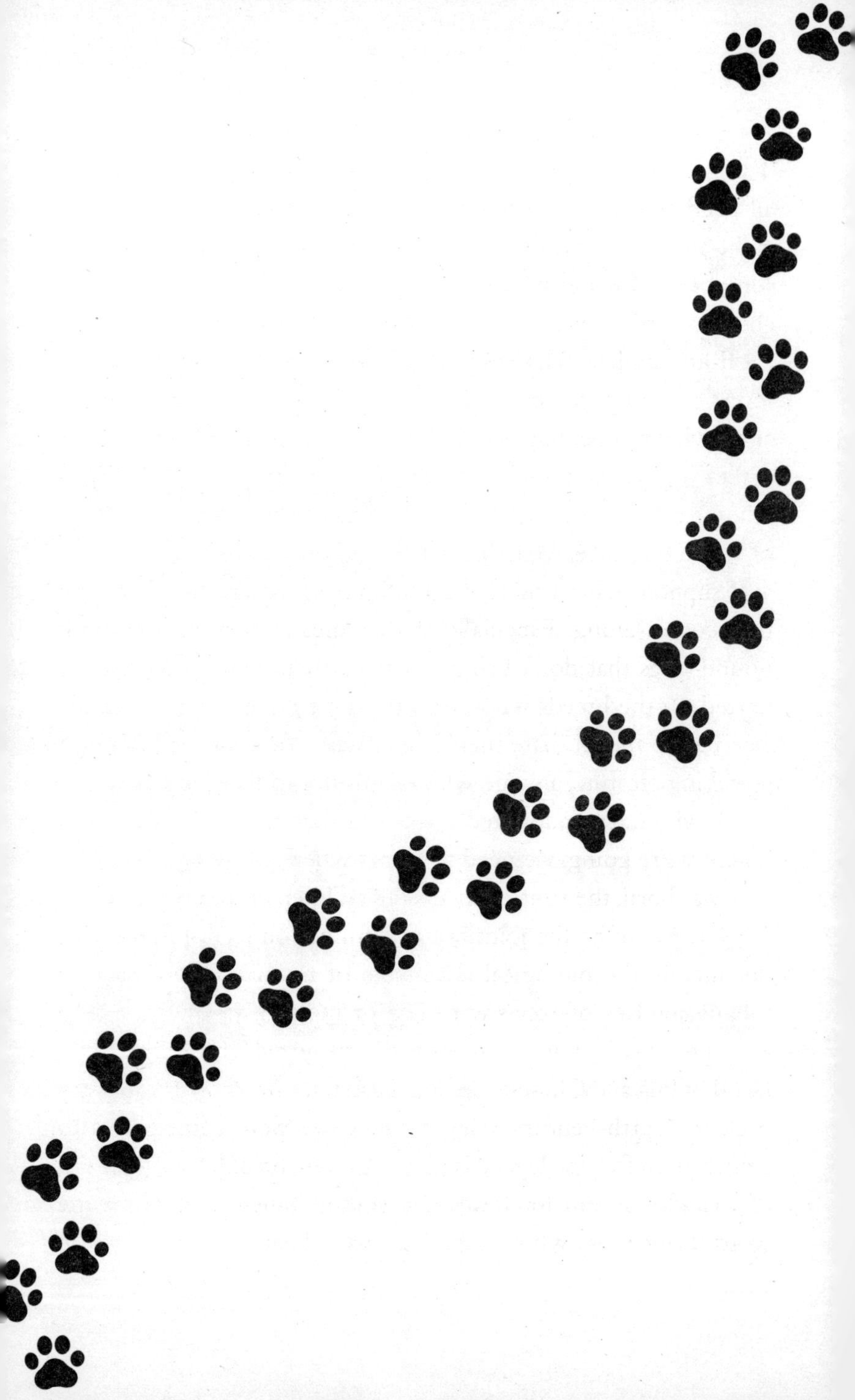

It is certainly true that all of us need to find our pack. Some of us are born into ours. Some of us find ours later in life. But we all need one. We need those we run with to help us run at the right speed, sometimes pulling us forwards when we need it, sometimes slowing us down. If you and your pack are aligned about what you want to chase (for example, the big evil ginger cat from number 27), then you will run in perfect step. However, if one of your pack decides for some reason to sniff the pavement at the vital moment and in doing so tangles legs with you, which makes you trip and roll headlong into a neighbour's bin, then you emerge covered in southern fried chicken and a pungent cocktail of warm bin juice. Well, that is obviously tricky to style out.

I suppose what I'm saying is, don't just accept the first pack that comes along. Especially if that means hanging out with hound-dogs that don't bring out the best in you (don't get me started on the breeds who demand to see your pedigree certificate before they'll share their chews with you), cats or that most terrifying creature, anyone who claims not to be a 'dog person'.

However, it's undoubtedly true that before we can work out where we're going, we need to know where we've been.

I was born, the runt of an accidental litter, in the late spring of 2019. It was to be the joint hottest summer on record in the UK, but luckily the biological advantage of my naturally capacious tongue and lack of excess warming fur, meant I was always able to keep pretty cool. I am a Pugese by heritage, which means I am a blend of Pug and Chinese Crested. I can trace my mother's ancestry back to fourth-century China, where we were companions to emperors. In fact, the legend is that Pugs were bred to have a pattern of wrinkles on our foreheads that is the Chinese symbol for the word 'prince'. In which case, as I have been known to say at cocktail parties, we are all, very much 'the barkist formerly known as Prince'. We've always had an association with royalty, with both Russia's Catherine the Great and Britain's Queen Victoria devoted companions to Pugs. My family likely came to England on the boats of Dutch traders at some point in the seventeenth century. I like to think it's where I've got my love of travel from, but it might also be because it works with my serious commitment to napping.

The first six months of my life were spent watching as my brothers and sisters, one by one, were adopted and left the litter. Perhaps some might have found this dispiriting, but I always knew that there was no hurry. At some point I would find my pack. I was always different to them. Every time a dog came on the television, I would stand up and bark. I knew that was where I wanted to get to one day. My influences have always been many and wide-ranging. For example, I am inspired by Lassie's open and frank communication style. By Toto's love of Oz. By Scooby Doo's unmatched detective skills. And by Lady Gaga's desire to make clothing out of meat.

And then, as 2019 came to a close, along came Holly. All the other pups had gone. I remember her gazing down at me and there was one word in my head: 'yes'. She reached down and lifted me up and I nuzzled into her neck. It was like one piece of a puzzle fitting into another. And with Holly was Luke. I had been worried that I would be placed with an overly hairy family, so it was such a relief to meet him. It was like looking in a mirror. Not everyone is lucky enough to be bald, so I was glad Luke was similarly blessed and would understand the burden that privilege brings. Holly and Luke have referred to me as reminding them of a 'Jim Henson creation', which I assume is some sort of high-end fashion thing. It was love at first sight and entirely mutual.

Holly and Luke also had small humans of their own, though by the time I arrived, they weren't newly hatched and already able to move, a little. Human infants have always been somewhat of a mystery to me. Puppies are, quite sensibly, really just small dogs. They might be a bit bouncier, wrigglier etc. but they are essentially just an adult dog but smaller. From what I can tell, human puppies in their infancy are more like a kind of jolly blob with a (sort of) human face. They can essentially do nothing for the first year. I assume the adult humans make them carry their faeces in a bag glued to them as some sort of punishment for this uselessness. It is a miracle that humanity exists at all, really. But I could see immediately how Holly and Luke were so generous with their love and it gave me hope that they might feel the same about snacks. So there it finally was: my pack.

After some backwards and forwards, I was named Peggy, after Holly's great grandmother. I had been workshopping some other potential names at the time, including Thor, Nautilus and The Devastator, but Peggy was great, too. Owning a family is a big responsibility for any dog, but I felt immediately at home with my new pack. Sometimes you just click with people. They liked putting food in my bowl. I liked it when they put food in my bowl. They really liked scratching my tummy. I really liked displaying my admittedly very fine tummy. It was just one of those mutually beneficial relationships.

They also, and I cannot stress how important this is, understood the absolutely immovable rule that is the cheese tax, whereby any human who visits the fridge for cheese must give the dog in their life a piece of cheese. I have heard about houses who refuse to pay the cheese tax and, to be honest, the thought genuinely scares me.

There was one odd quirk about them, which was that Holly and Luke sometimes forgot to tuck me into the big bed where we were all supposed to sleep. But I'd always notice and make sure I was there, in my place in the middle of them, head on the pillow by morning. I have occasionally been accused of 'snoring like a chainsaw,' but I can neither confirm nor deny that.

The key thing was that the whole pack was all aligned with what we wanted, together. I was determined to do whatever it took to become a beacon of hope and inclusivity, to show that whoever we are, wherever we're from and whatever we look like, we are all truly beautiful and deserving of love. And they would follow me around picking up my poos and putting them in a little bag.

Lesson 2: Learn to fetch your dreams

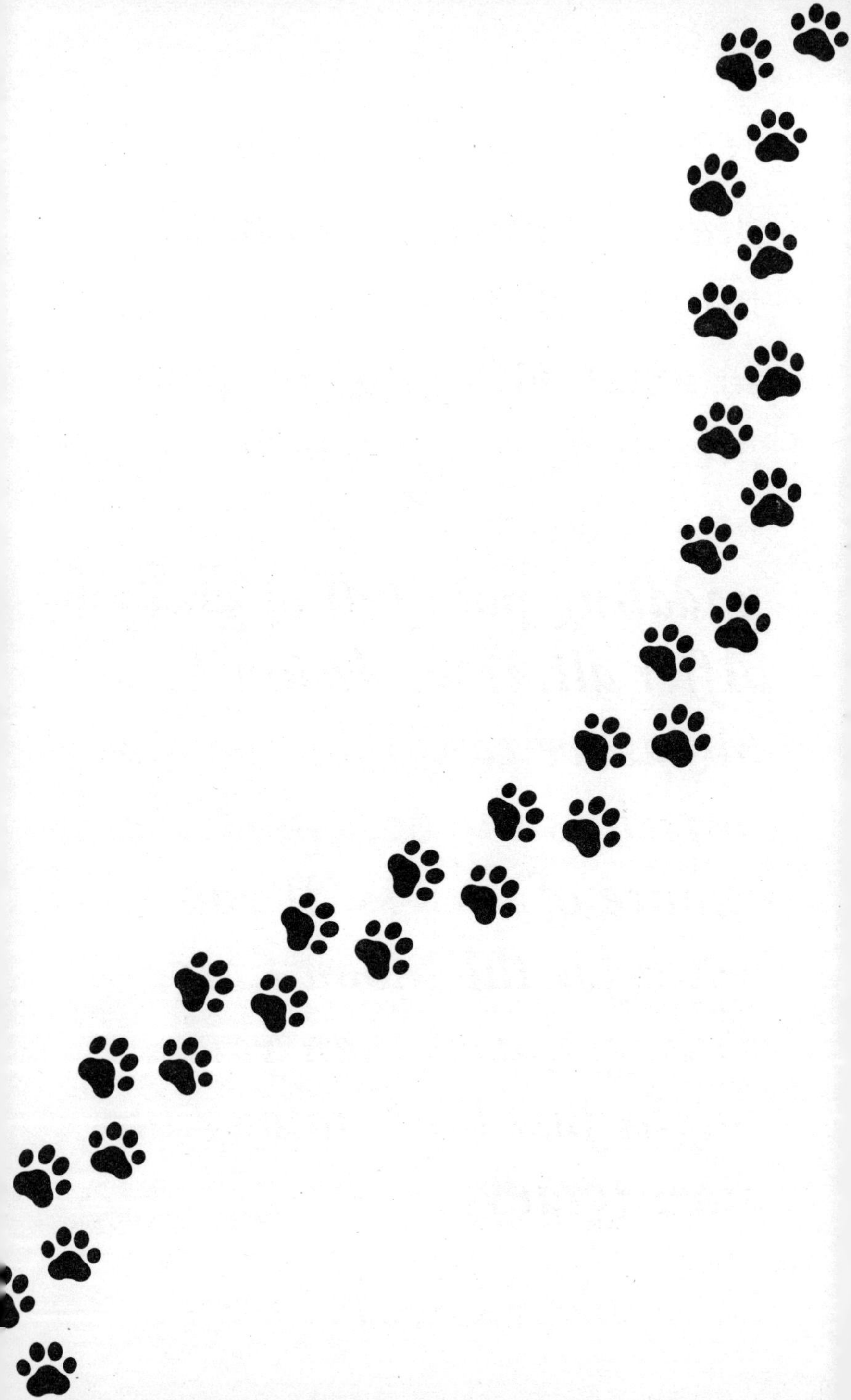

'Our dreams should be a place where we allow the biggest of potential futures to exist. Why not let your dream be a sausage the size of a Shetland pony, or a paddling pool full of gravy? After all, if we dream as big as we can, then we give ourselves the best possible chance of success. If you reach for the moon (large sausage), well then you might just land among the stars (gravy).'

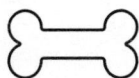

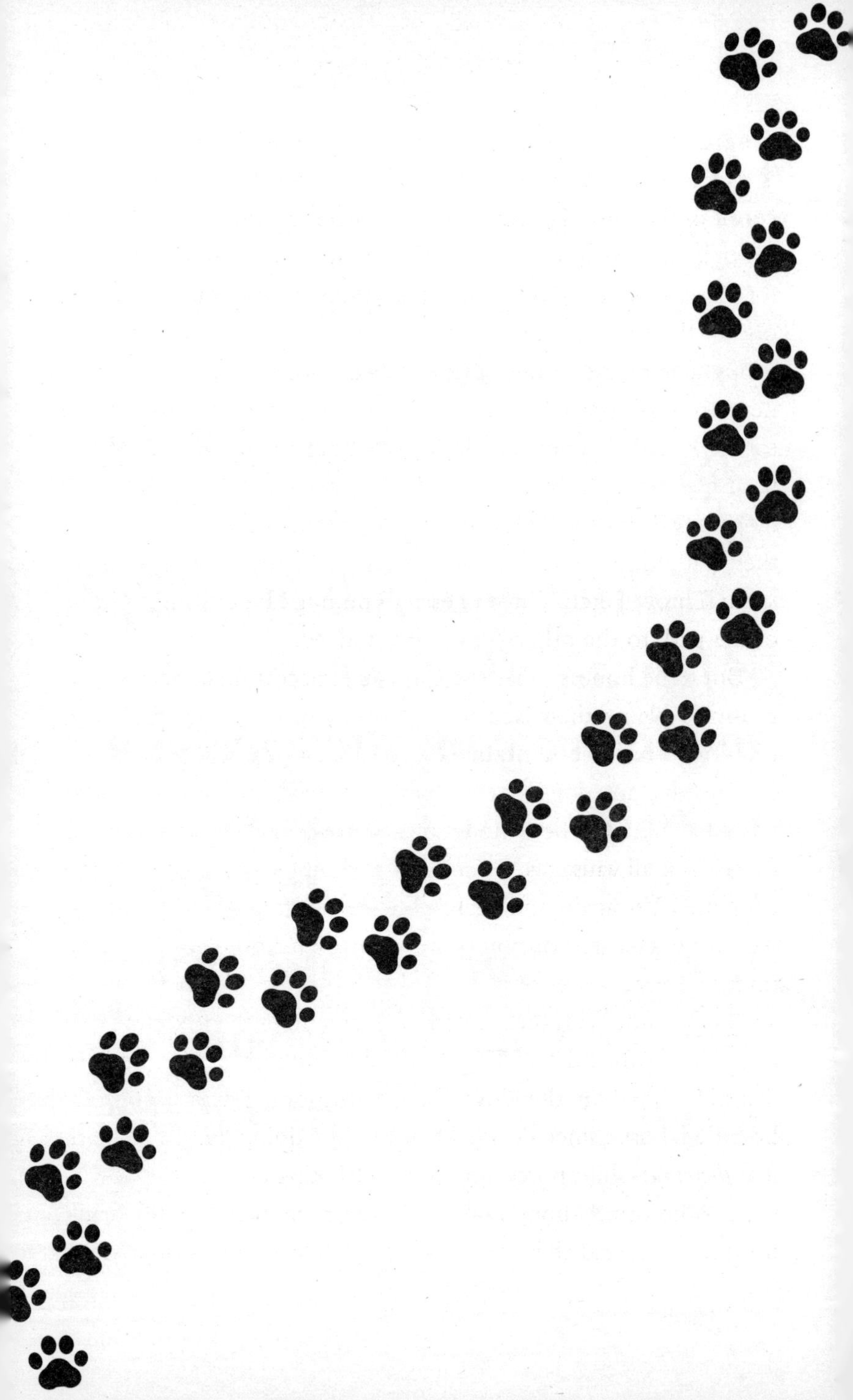

I hope you'll forgive me for noting at this point that humans are bad at holding on to what matters to them. Very bad. I've lost count of the number of times I've returned a human's special ball or stick, smiling and saying 'Make sure you take better ca…' only for them to fling it away and the whole cycle begins again. It's one of the most mysterious things about humans. I have always thought it reveals something essential about your psyche. This need to fling your most important things away from you. I dread to think what happens to those poor humans without a dog in their life. Presumably they fling their stick or ball away and that's it. No more stick or ball for them. Or perhaps they throw it and then pathetically chase it themselves. Then throw it again. And again. Throw. Fetch. Throw. Fetch. Running alone from one side of the park to the other. A sad story indeed.

But to be honest, what else can you expect from a species who routinely blame their lack of homework on a dog having eaten it? Now, I have certainly never eaten anyone's academic work. And nor has any dog I've ever spoken to. And, unless their home-work happened to be a model of a motte-and-bailey castle made from cocktail sausages, I very much doubt it has ever actually happened. Yet again and again you see it referenced. My advice would be: take responsibility for your own homework, or lack thereof. Leave us out of it.

It's the same with their manners. I remember the first time one of my humans did *THAT* in the tall, white, porcelain upright drinking bowl in the downstairs bathroom. I was absolutely horrified. I have since decided that they are doing *THAT* to mark it as *their* tall, white, porcelain upright drinking bowl in the down-stairs bathroom. Although I am yet to ever see them actually drink from it — instead they insist on doing their business in it. Wild.

But even so, it is just another thing that reveals a deep tension at the heart of the human psyche. And that extends to your dreams and goals.

Right from puppyhood, I knew that I was setting my course for Hollywood. I would sit on the sofa and watch all the greats — De Niro, Pacino, the Churchill Insurance Dog — and work out ways that I could beg borrow and steal technique from them. And then I would implement it in my day-to-day life. When it was time for walkies, I would look at Holly as if I had never encountered the concept before. Or I would jump onto the sofa as if she had just said it was time for us to sit and watch television. If I found the bag of dog biscuits and dragged it out of the cupboard, ripping the bag to shreds and distributing a slurry of half-eaten biscuits and drool all over the kitchen floor, I would respond to their questions as to what had happened with a look of such puzzled innocence that they assumed there must have been a break-in. Hell, when I played dead, they damn near broke out the defibrillators! At every stage, I had my eye on the prize. And this is a key lesson I want to impart to you. Make sure your dreams are big enough.

Someone once said to me (the extremely famous director, Steven Spielberg) 'There is no special effects budget in your dreams' and that really resonated with me. You don't have to let your dreams be constrained by the petty day-to-day concerns that limit most of the rest of our lives.

You may have heard the phrase 'the world is your oyster'. I dislike this saying immensely. Of all the things for the world to be, I would say my least favourite would be a small rubbery globule that smells strongly of whale sick. Honestly, it's like Poseidon has hocked up a phlegm wad and then somehow convinced rich people to eat it as a joke. You know who I bet loves oysters? Cats. Enough said.

But the *sentiment* I very much agree with. Our dreams should be a place where we allow the biggest of potential futures to exist. Why not let your dream be a sausage the size of a Shetland pony, or a paddling pool full of gravy? After all, if we dream as big as we can, then we give ourselves the best possible chance of success.

If you reach for the moon (large sausage), well then you might just land among the stars (gravy).

If I'd allowed myself to believe that my world would forever be the same charming but remote corner of the north-east of England, then I would never have won my first award, I would never have starred on the small screen and then the big screen. We must, all of us, fight to keep our horizons as wide as possible. Everyone's dream will be different. For some, it might be making their family proud, for others it's making a difference in the world. For some, it might be running hog wild in a Toby Carvery and eating so much meat you need to sleep for a week. These are all noble ambitions.

But reaching your goals isn't easy. Truly hard things take dedication. And I'd be wrong not to acknowledge that we're not all starting from the same place. Believe you can overcome the obstacles, acknowledge your privileges. We don't all get the same opportunities or talent. I know not everyone can have a magnificent tongue like mine. Indeed, it's taken me many years of dedication to grow mine to its true potential. But we all have our own inner tongue. (Again, this is a metaphor, I know this isn't anatomically true. Although someone once told me that a snail's foot is its tongue. So, if you're a snail and reading this, probably with your intestines or something — go you!)

But here's the key thing. Sometimes to get to your ultimate dream, you have to be flexible. You have to be willing to walk a different path. Sometimes you have to be prepared to let go of something that seems like it really matters at the time. Because even doors that close, often have a little flap for cats to use that you can get back in through.

All things — sticks, balls, cats balancing on the wall acting like they own the bloody place, will pass. Life is change. Sometimes fetching the stick can feel like the right thing to do because we are all scared of change. But we need to accept change into our lives. Sometimes we have the stick. Sometimes we don't. But our self-worth does not come from the stick. We are a good dog whether we have the stick or not.

Letting go of the stick means that we can pick up the ball, or the treat or even the mouldering fox poo. As we release the stick, we open up a space (not just in our mouths) for renewal and transformation. When we are intentional about what we fetch, we find we aren't just repeating the same old patterns. It means that when we do fetch, we can reconnect with it as a joyful act of self. We are fetching our dreams.

You won't realise how much energy you have been wasting worrying about fetching. Humming away in the background, taking up space you could be using on other things. Buddhism teaches us that cultivating non-attachment is the only way to find true peace and fulfilment. The stick is there. You value the stick. But you do not need to possess the stick. If another dog goes and tries to get the stick, you do not need to chase after them shouting, 'My stick, hey, my stick, hey, my stick, you monster!' as your human sprints after you, calling, 'Peggy, noooooooooo!'

For example.

Lesson 3: How to dogifest

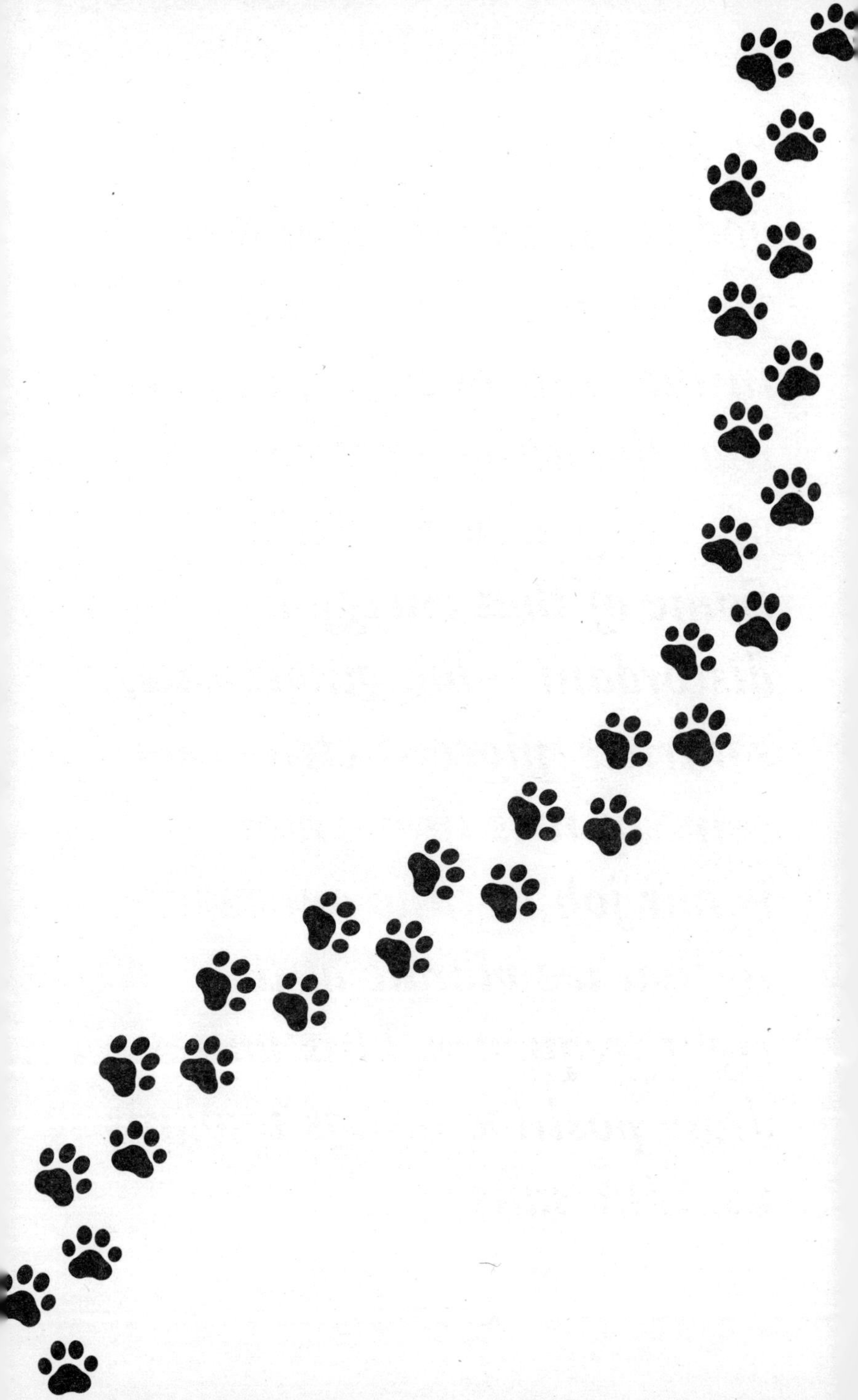

'I would like to note that god is an anagram of dog, if you want to find significance in that sort of thing. I believe that the universe is composed of energy and vibration. Some of that energy is discordant – big ginger cats, squirrels, pigeons etc. – and some of it is in harmony. It is our job to tune ourselves so that we vibrate at the right frequency. This will draw positive things towards us. Like sausages.'

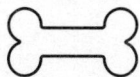

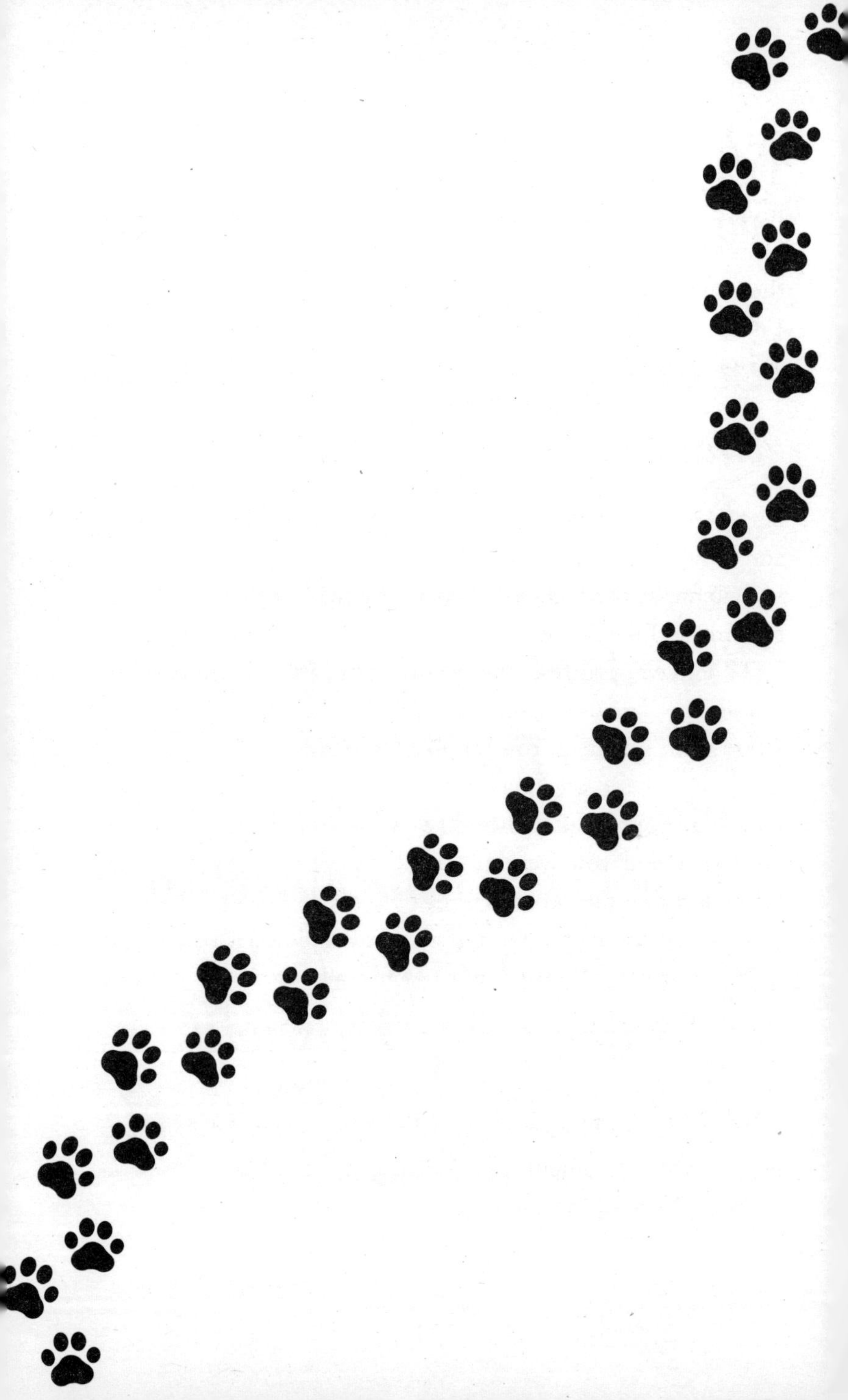

Much as nobody knows why the human brings the strange paper rectangles and pushes them through the slot in the front door, only that we must scare them away as quickly as possible by loudly shouting, 'Hey, hey, go away. My house. My house!', there are large parts of life that are essentially a mystery. Though I don't subscribe to any one religion, I would describe myself as a very spiritual dog.

I would also like to note that god is an anagram of dog, if you want to find significance in that sort of thing. I believe that the universe is composed of energy and vibration. Some of that energy is discordant — big ginger cats, squirrels, pigeons etc. — and some of it is in harmony. It is our job to tune ourselves so that we vibrate at the right frequency. This will draw positive things towards us. Like sausages.

When we dogifest, there are a number of different techniques we can use to be clear about the things we want to attract into our lives. You might consider using what is called a vision board and create a collage of images and words that best represent your goals. So perhaps you could place a picture of yourself when you were at your happiest and most confident. Or asleep, that's good too.

Or how about the word 'resilient'. People say that a lot these days. Or if you're unsure what you really want, I recommend choosing a classic. How about a giant bowl full of so many sausages that the sausages are overflowing out of the bowl and around the bowl is a kind of moat of glistening sausages? Or perhaps you could keep a journal. Here, make sure to use active, present-tense statements like 'I attract success', 'I am confident' or 'Sausages flow to me easily'.

I know many other A-list stars are fans of a technique called scripting. This is where you write out vivid, detailed scenarios where success has *already happened*. Naturally, this is harder for me, as my handwriting is not my strongest point (we all have our failings, never be afraid to admit yours — as long as it not refusing to share cheese). Still, if you don't like your handwriting, do hire a secretary. I like to keep Luke and Holly busy with tasks like this. It's important for them to feel needed.

So you could write, or ask your assistant to write, 'It is a beautiful summer morning, I wake in my dream home. From the kitchen the smell of freshly brewed coffee comes. I walk through the sun-drenched kitchen and out into the garden, where the sunlight glints on my swimming pool.' Or perhaps, 'I am awoken from my deep, refreshing sleep by the sound of the butcher's delivery truck doors falling open and spilling the contents onto the road', or even, 'After twenty years of the squirrel vs pigeon wars, both sides have decided to bow to their canine overlords.'

However you do it, the important thing is to keep them vivid, present tense and rich in sensory detail. Repetition can be your friend here. Perhaps you could write your goals three times in the morning, six times in the afternoon and nine times just before bed. Or just before or after any of your twenty-seven naps. I have a very clear memory of dogifesting two images. The first was me on a red carpet with camera flashes going off. The second was the HMV icon of a dog and a gramophone but with me as the dog. Both of them happened. (And if you think that second one is oddly specific and can't be true, I have nothing to say to you. Except you should consider getting out more. Get some culture.)

This detailed visualisation, combined with regular meditation practice and a disciplined sense of gratitude will put you well on the way to dogifesting the future that you want and deserve.

The important thing is that these goals are tangible and specific. There's no point having the goal, 'have a happy life'. But if you make it specific — *I want to shout at pigeons at least twice a day* — then you are far more likely to achieve your goals.

Lesson 4: Shake it off

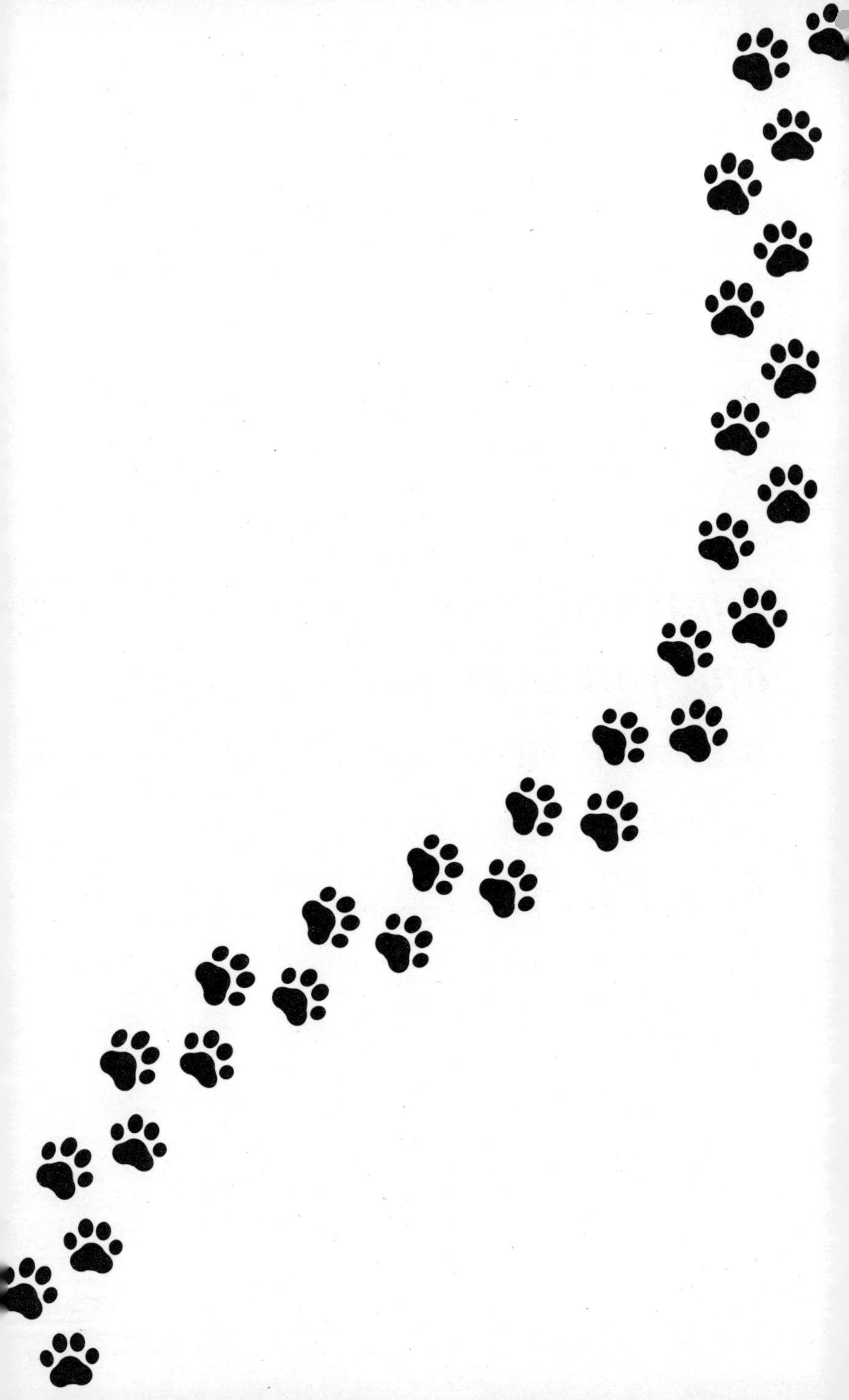

'The stick that is too long and feels like a tree trunk? That will one day be the one you bear aloft easily, bashing into the shins of any humans foolish enough to get in your way.'

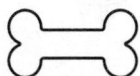

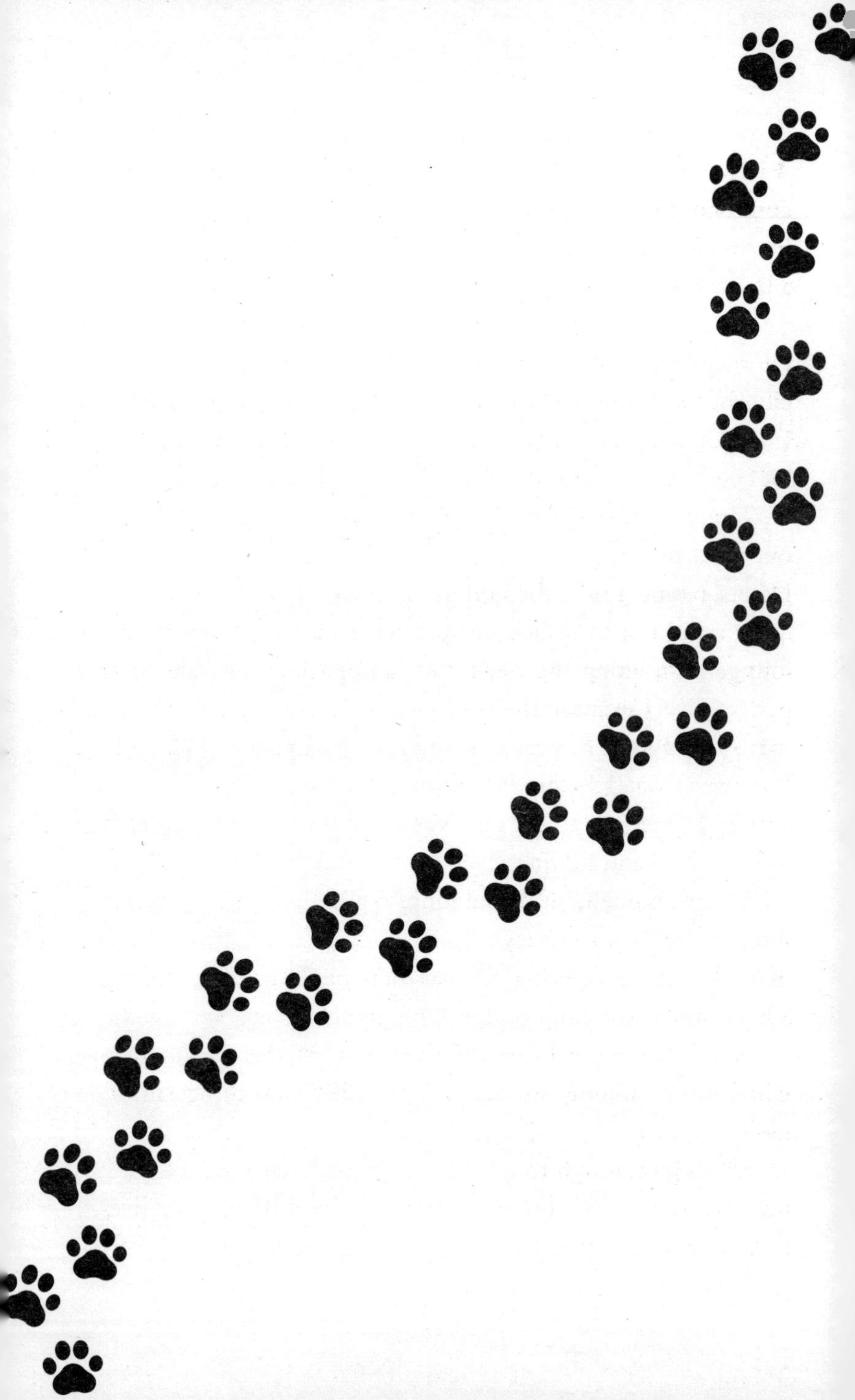

was once lounging by a lake at a party in the Hamptons where it was rumoured Taylor Swift was attending. Now don't be confused. Like Christopher Wren, Florence Nightingale, Mick Herron, Ethan Hawke, Russel Crowe and Frasier Crane, Taylor is a human with a bird for a surname. Not an actual bird.

I adore Taylor. We've got a lot in common after all — both international style icons, equally at home in the country or the big city, she's got a great voice, I've got a bark that can split the night. I was enjoying the party when I finally saw her, approaching my lounger and talking a friend through a bad date she'd been on.

'Honestly, they're saying I go on too many dates. That I stay out too late. I'm getting it from every direction. Players, playing. Haters, hating. I'm at the end of my tether.'

In a bid not to invade her privacy, I jumped down from the lounger, ran along the deck and jumped into the lake with a perfect dive. I swam in the cool, clear water, grateful for my aerodynamic build. If you can call a potato aerodynamic. Which I do. But even a water-loving Pugese like me has their limits, and after a while it was time to get out. My beloved Taylor was still talking to her friend and I didn't want her to think I was eavesdropping.

At that moment, in desperation to alert her to my presence, I shook myself with a series of long, glorious shakes, firing droplets of cool water all over her. She sat there blinking, her eyes bright, a huge smile blooming on her now drenched face.

I don't know, but I think in that moment, that joyful, freeing, whole-body shimmy, she might just have found the germ of an idea.

We all go through tough times. We experience hardships. It is how we respond to these setbacks that will define our lives. I think about the times I've been left at home for upwards of ten minutes on my own. Or been forced to roll on the floor to scratch my own back instead of receiving back rubs.

We can't control that things that happen to us. But we can control how we think about them and then respond to them. We can wallow, blaming everyone else for what has happened to us. We all meet people who do this. But it is the quickest way to unhappiness and a lack of fulfilment. When we focus on things we can't control, we remove power from our lives. And being fabulous is about increasing our power wherever we can. Put it this way, when you go for a walk, you could choose to focus on the lead. After all, from one perspective, it is controlling you. Stopping you from going where you want to go, sniffing what you want to sniff, weeing on all the things that need weeing on. The lead could come to symbolise all sorts of things. If only you didn't have the damned thing around your neck, imagine what you could achieve. But try this thought experiment.

Imagine for a moment if an alien came down to Earth and decided to try and work out who was the dominant species on our planet. In the park, they would watch as small, furry creatures on four legs at one end of a lead walked and ran around tall, two-legged ones. From time to time, the two-legged ones would reach down and pick up the faeces of the four-legged ones and place it in a bag. At home, the two-legged creature would place food in a receptacle for the four-legged one, before leaving to go and work at 'The Orifice'. (Note to editor, please fact check this.)

Meanwhile, the four-legged creature sleeps in their basket, perhaps gently chews a toy provided by the two-legged one, before the two-legged creature then returns, puts more food out, takes them out on the lead and picks up more of their faeces and puts it in a bag. After several days, the alien would conclude that it was the four-legged emperors who were clearly the ruling class. And they would, of course, be correct. After all, as a working definition for power, identifying which one picks up the other one's poo is about as good a definition as I can think of. So suddenly that lead? Well what would you do to make sure the most important thing in your life didn't run away. You'd probably come up with something that looked very much like a dog lead wouldn't you? Suddenly that lead isn't such a negative. The same lead. But how you're feeling about it is totally changed.

You can try this method in every part of your life:

Instead of saying 'You never listen,' try, 'I feel heard when we both stay present.'

Instead of saying 'That's wrong,' try 'You're on the right track — let's adjust this part.' Instead of 'Why are you sent to curse me, tiny, furry tiger demon?' you could say, 'Nice kitty, please don't step too near.'

Remember, there are no bad ideas, just opportunities to do things better. Instead of failing, you're putting one paw in front of another on the road towards success. The task that right now feels too hard? It's challenging and helping you to get better. The stick that is too long and feels like a tree trunk? That will one day be the one you bear aloft easily, bashing into the shins of any humans foolish enough to get in your way.

All of us have so many metaphorical dog leads in our lives (I actually also have a lot of literal ones, as I like to match my lead with my outfit. I haven't actually counted recently but I want to say a hundred? Give or take.)

When we learn to reframe our hardships, we learn to leave them behind. We do not dwell on disappointments and let them shape our lives.

Instead, we can find a way to accommodate our past, take ownership of our mistakes and shake them off.

It is then we truly come into our power.

And if that still doesn't work? Go back to basics. Take a shower. Relax in the sensation of the water. And when you're done? Don't bother with that ridiculous human invention, the towel. It was made to steal your joy. Instead, don't be tempted to drip dry but do as I always recommend — shake it off. You'll either feel much, much better, or you'll put your back out doing it and be in too much pain to think about whatever was bothering you before.

Lesson 5: Today is going to be your day

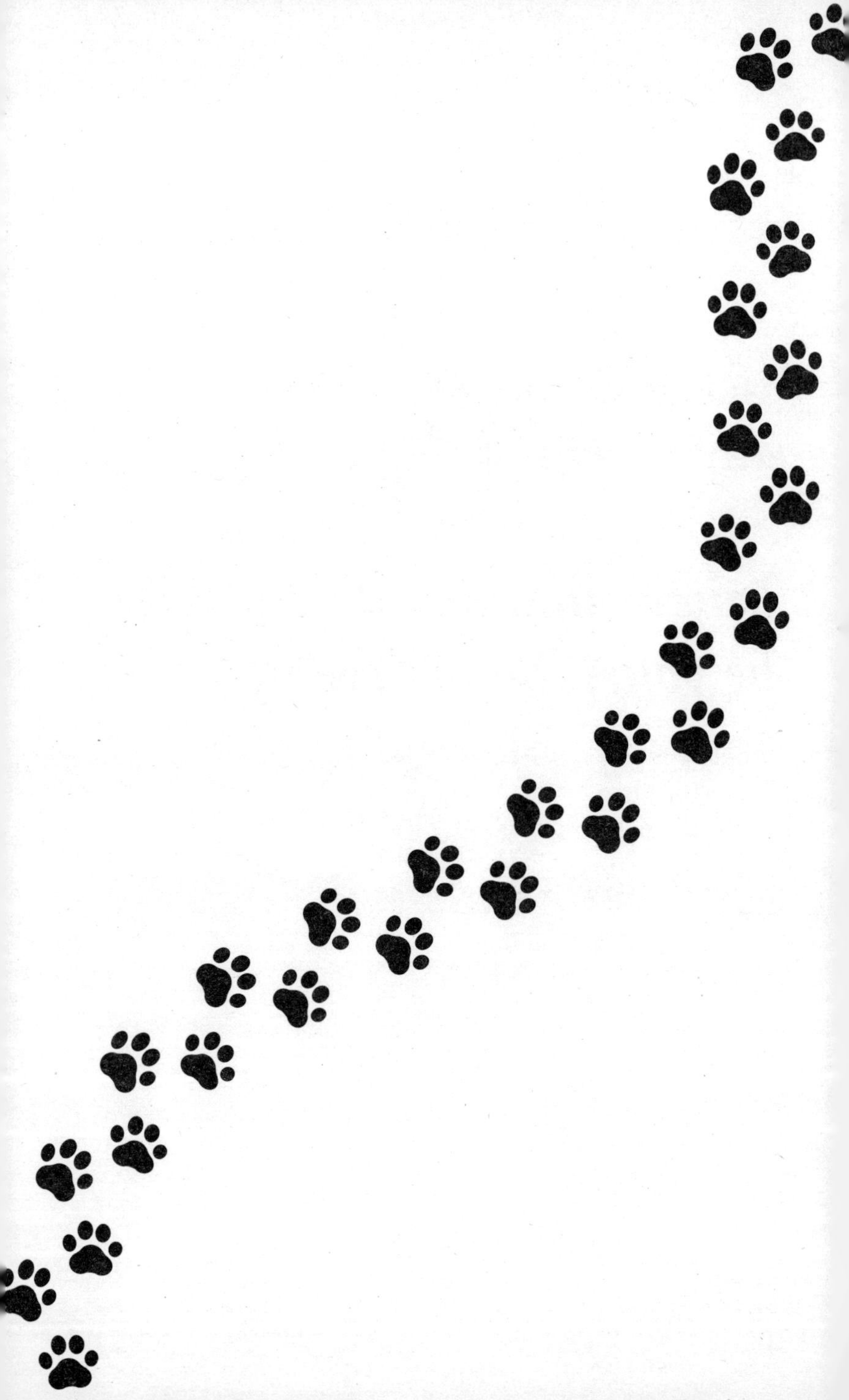

'I always believed that one day it would be my day. And I want you to always believe that one day it will be yours. So believe in yourself. Be kind to yourself. And always carry snacks. And your time will come.'

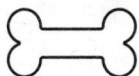

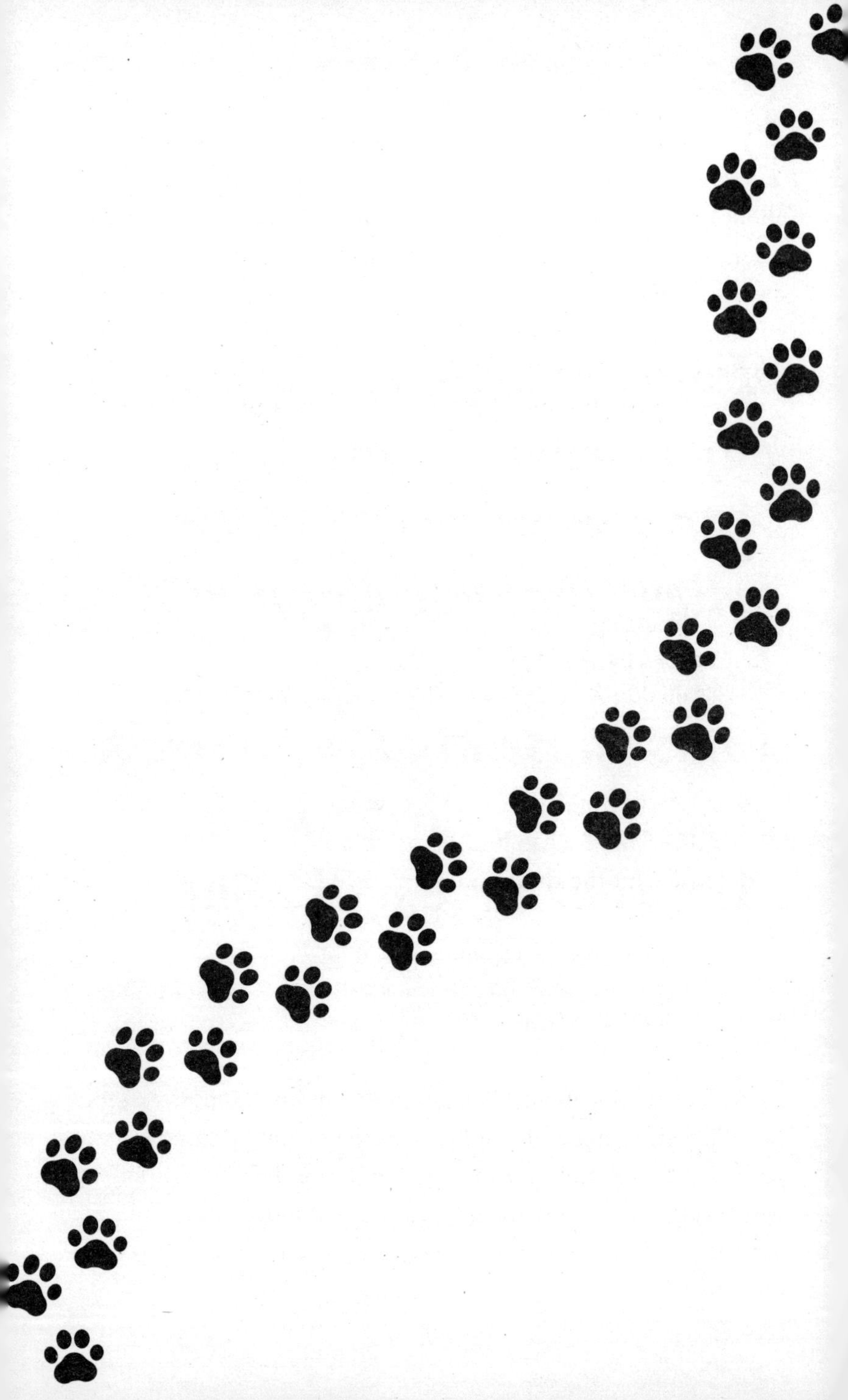

B efore we get going on this chapter, I just want to be honest and say I've always thought there was something slightly 'off' about the expression 'every dog has their day'. There is an implied 'even' in there. As if every *dog* having their moment somehow lowers the overall value of *anyone* having one. It's a phrase used to comfort humans. 'Look, if even every dog has their day, then you, a human, definitely will.'

I was uneasy about this, so I thought I'd look up the dictionary definition for dog. The first bit is fine:

> **Domesticated canine** — *A four-legged domesticated mammal (Canis familiaris), descended from wolves, commonly kept as pets and trained for work like guarding, hunting or companionship.*
>
> Second bit. Also fine:
>
> **Male dog** — *Specifically refers to an adult male of the species.*

Though I would note that the word for the female of the species is also quite a bad insult in all human languages but hey ho. Then we hit the third meaning:

> **Informal uses** — *A contemptible or unattractive person, e.g., 'You dirty dog', Something inferior or lousy, e.g., 'That movie was a dog'.*

As I say, it's not about settling scores. This book is positive vibes only. All I'm saying is, if you heard someone saying someone was your best friend with one breath, then using their name to mean everything that's bad with the next… You'd judge them wouldn't you? What would you think if you were at brunch and on the next table you heard someone say 'Oh, I love Janice, she's my best friend' and then with the next breath, 'Oh my god, don't go and see that movie, it's a total Janice.' Would you think that person was a nice person? A good person? A trustworthy person?

While I'm here — a 'dog eat dog world'! Seriously? We might chase each other. We definitely bite each other sometimes. But there is a very long list of foods I'd choose before I got to a fellow pooch. And the 'doghouse' is where you get sent when you've done something wrong? Do you know what *we* call 'the doghouse'? Home.

And why, if something has become bad, has it gone to the dogs? As if dogs invaded and made something bad. Whereas actually, the only time something would ever 'go' to us would be if humans destroyed or abandoned it first. Seriously, when in the annals of history have you come across a story where dogs have invaded and taken territory by force from humans. 'Oh, did you hear about the Roman Empire? Turns out it fell because an army of Schnauzers sacked the capital.' So, actually, what's normally happened is that humans have messed up and abandoned somewhere and it's up to the dogs to move in and fix it.

And while we're here, why does a *dog's dinner* mean something looks bad? Ninety-nine per cent of the time, who makes the dog's dinner?! You do. That's like two insults piled on top of each other. First you prepare a dinner that you know looks bad. Which means it's deliberate. Then you use how bad our dinner looks as a metaphor for other things that also look bad. Talk about a red flag. That's hardly aspirational for us, is it? And just a reminder that not all of us have fleas. So lying down with us is fine. And they're only fleas anyway. If the price of 'lying down' with an amazing friend is a few fleas, well I've got news for you, maybe you need to open your mind a bit.

But like I say, I like to look on the bright side. So as for 'working like a dog', at least you admit that we work hard.

While we're here, we really need to have a talk about honesty. Because pretty much every male dog I know, at some point in their early life, was told they were going to 'the park'. But instead was taken to a building with bright white rooms, rows of chairs with people carrying odd crates with hamsters or cats inside, with hallways that smelled of antiseptic and other dogs. And what happened in this strange place? They (and excuse my frankness here) had their testicles removed. Yes, you read that correctly. Then, to compound the shame, they had a cone placed around their neck, presumably to signal to other dogs that this has happened. If this scene had taken place in *Game of Thrones* this would be one of the most shocking scenes ever broadcast. But instead it is entirely commonplace. Entirely unremarked upon.

I know what you're going to say, that I should 'let sleeping dogs lie'. Well, that one I won't argue with.

Sorry, I went off on one there. What I want to say is that I remember, all those years before anyone even knew I wanted to be a film star, I always believed that one day it would be my day. And I want you to always believe that one day it will be yours. So believe in yourself. Be kind to yourself. And always carry snacks. And your time will come. Because in spite of all of these human-on-dog insults. We forgive you. We love you. We lick you.

And us dogs, we don't sit around worrying about the passage of time. We know our moment will come. I once went to an outdoor production of *Hamlet*. To tell the truth it was very disappointing — two hours of people talking to each other, and ABSOLUTELY NO HAM ANYWHERE. There was one good bit with a skull where I thought they might talk more about bones and digging but they just went back to messing about with swords. But I do remember one line: *the readiness is all*.

It makes me wonder if I've concentrated too much on my film and TV work. Maybe the stage is calling — because after all, every dog will have their day.

And yes, you too *will* have your day and you know who the loudest cheerleader will be when that day comes?

Us.

Lesson 6: Live in the now

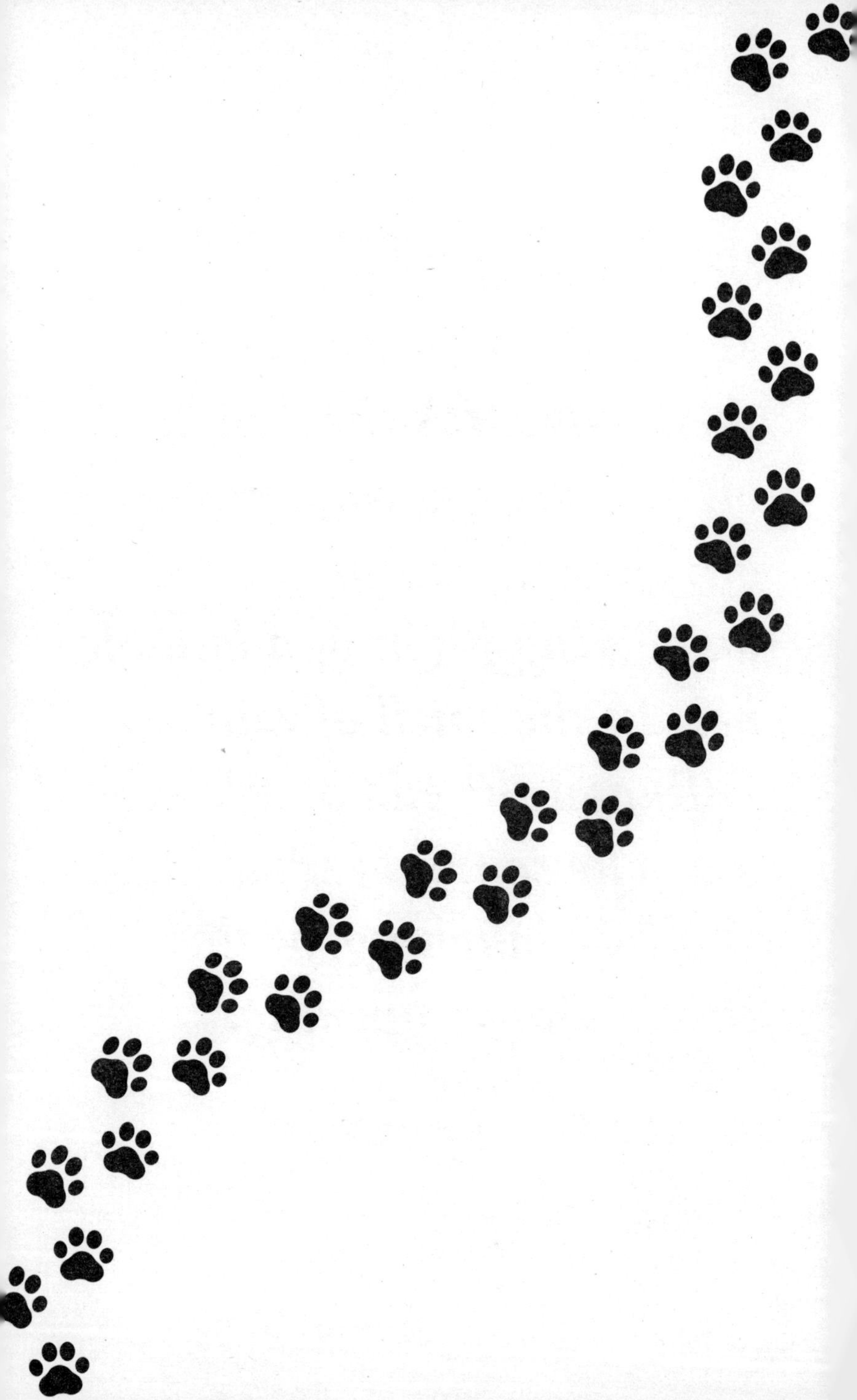

'The past and future essentially take care of themselves. It's the middle bit you need to concentrate on. Take joy in the wandering flight of a bumble bee. In the smell of rain falling at the end of a hot day. The sound of someone you love laughing, or the cheese drawer opening.'

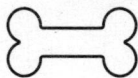

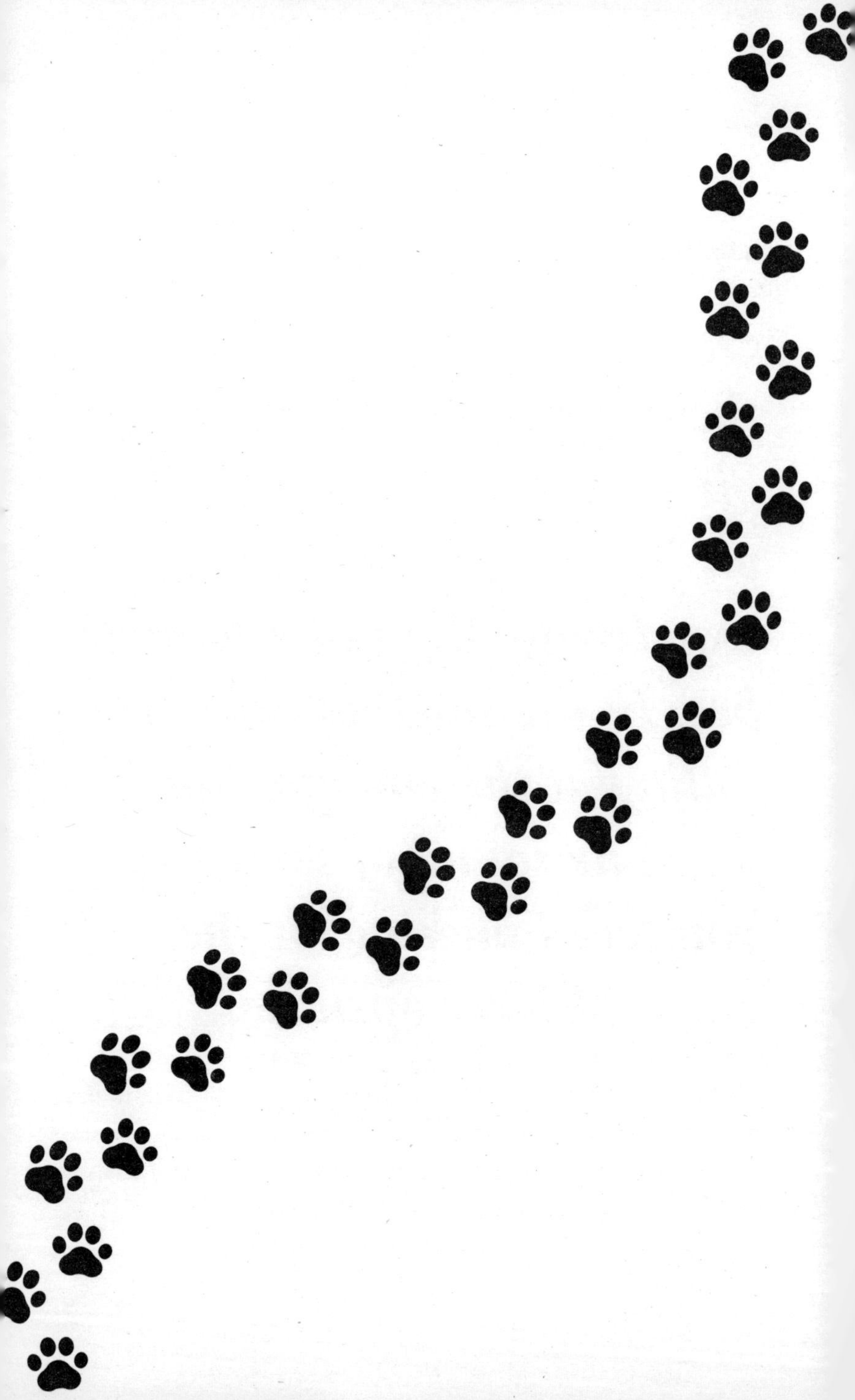

There have been times, not so much in recent years, when I have briefly been left to my own devices. In the hustle and bustle of the celebrity lifestyle, chance would be a fine thing! During these moments, it can be tempting to imagine that your humans have left forever. As you wander around the house, checking the rooms in case they are simply hiding, or perhaps have got stuck behind the sofa (again). Or in case they have left you two breakfasts today (like that one magical time they did — Two Breakfasts Day remains one of my best days ever).

Left alone, I know what it's like for terrible thoughts to creep in. You imagine all of the ways that they could have got lost out there without you. If you're being totally honest, are you even sure they know their way back from the park without you pulling them in the right direction? Perhaps a malign squirrel, or that massive ginger cat at number 27 has tempted them into some danger, as you always suspected was their plan? Or perhaps they have accidentally become involved in some sort of organised crime situation and been relocated with new identities in a nondescript town hundreds of miles away? A strange place, with smells you will never smell and parks you will never visit. Or perhaps aliens have taken them up into their craft to try and understand humanity? After all, wouldn't that make sense? If you were an alien seeking to understand a new civilisation, you would pick the very best of humans, your humans.

Any dogs reading will recognise those long, lonely minutes as you pace and circle the kitchen floor, perhaps from time to time offering tiny howls of quiet concern. Until, suddenly, they return! And you bound towards them, all that fear and worry melting away like an ice cube under a blowtorch. The joy of their return is all that matters. A huge, overleaping warmth, like the sun rising after the darkest, coldest of nights. And nothing else matters. Not the fact they weren't there in the past, not the fact they might go away again in the future. In this blazing, infinite present they are here and you are here and that is all that matters.

'Yesterday is history, tomorrow is a mystery, but today is a gift. That's why it's called the present.' I thought this was going to be a quote by someone meaningful at first. But it turns out it's just from *Kung Fu Panda*. I have nothing against the franchise, though I remain slightly uneasy about the trend for animated animals taking work from real, live ones. With nice mohawks and an abundance of nipples. There might have been *101 Dalmatians* but the animation resulted in precisely zero paycheques for any actual dogs.

It's hard enough trying to find a good role at the best of times. So then you factor in all the roles where the dog is actually a cartoon voiced by a human. Probably playing some sort of scrappy mongrel who gets drawn into a series of adventures where he ultimately realises that he needs to be true to himself, not try and pretend he's someone that he isn't. You see? I've watched plenty of these cartoon dog films. I mean, what's a girl to do on a transatlantic flight? I get it. Those films are touching and uplifting but how many actual dogs are employed? Zero. Don't get me wrong – I love an animated legend, Snoopy or Muttley, Pluto or Dogtanian...but I'm delighted to see some live action remakes now with actual canine stars. All this CGI is amazing, but can a computer capture the joyful slobber of a happy hound in full technicolor? (If you read this and would like to have a meeting about *The Dogfather, Bark to the Future,* or any other original screenplay ideas, please do contact my agent.)

The lesson? The main thing to focus on is living in the now. If you are a human with a dog in your life, you'll know the truth of this. We dogs are like an unstoppable force, dragging our humans into the present. It is the biggest difference between us and you. The time you waste thinking about things that have already happened but you can't change, or things that might never happen. You lose sight of what's actually happening, now, right in front of you. You can't enjoy the tummy rub because you're worried that at some point it will stop. You can't be grateful for the sausage falling from the table because you're too busy thinking about the time you thought a sausage had fallen from the table but it was actually a crayon but you still ate it and then forgot until it was time to do a poo and gave yourself a right fright. For example.

What I'm saying is that the past and future essentially take care of themselves. It's the middle bit you need to concentrate on. Take joy in the wandering flight of a bumble bee. In the smell of rain falling at the end of a hot day. The sound of someone you love laughing, or the cheese drawer opening.

More than anything, if I had one piece of advice, it would be this: find something in your life that makes you feel like dogs do when their humans come home.

Lesson 7: Walkies!

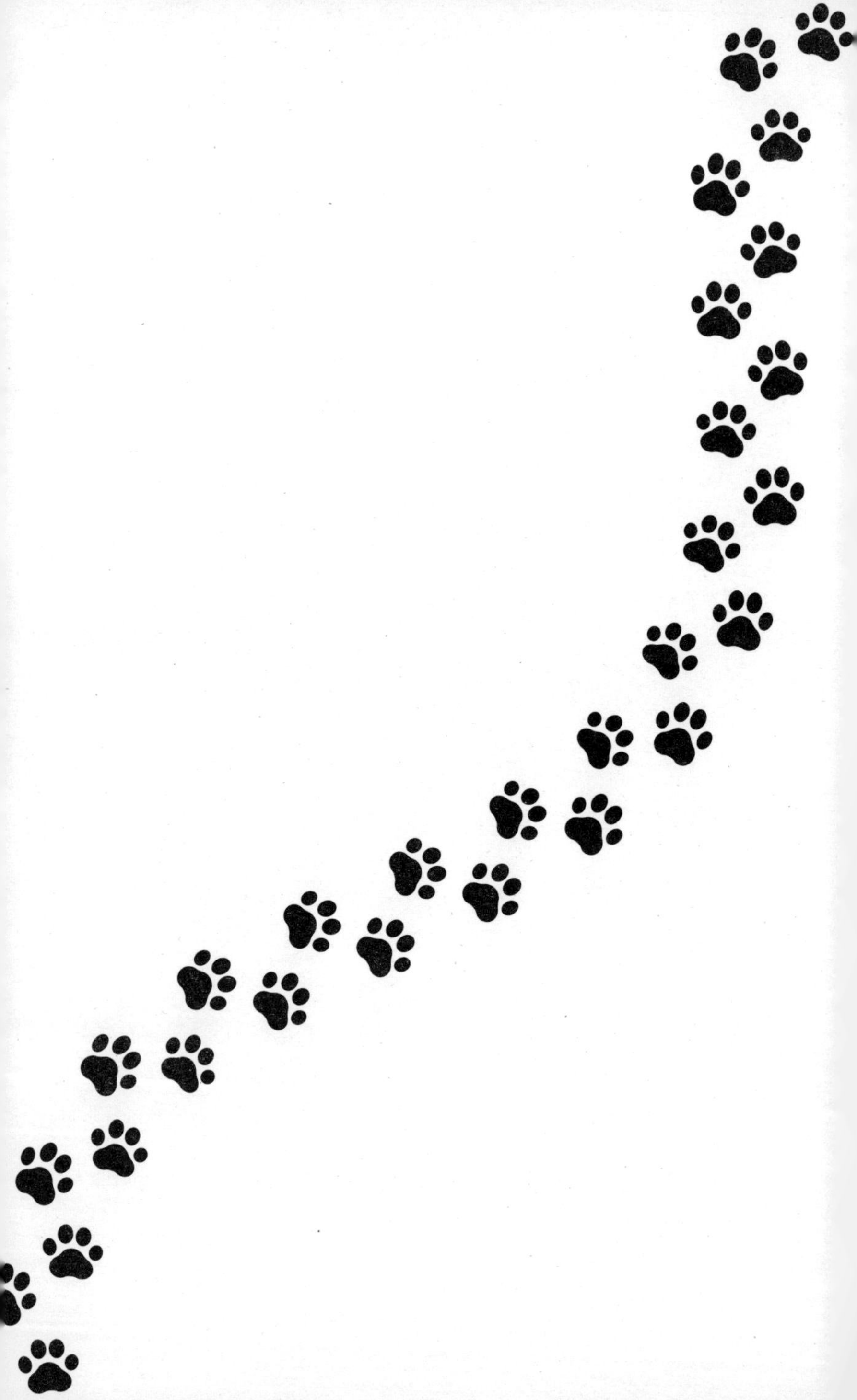

'Before you start a walk, take a moment to concentrate on your breath, to feel your body and what it is telling you. Unless it's telling you to sit back down again – that's not what we need right now.'

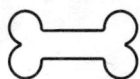

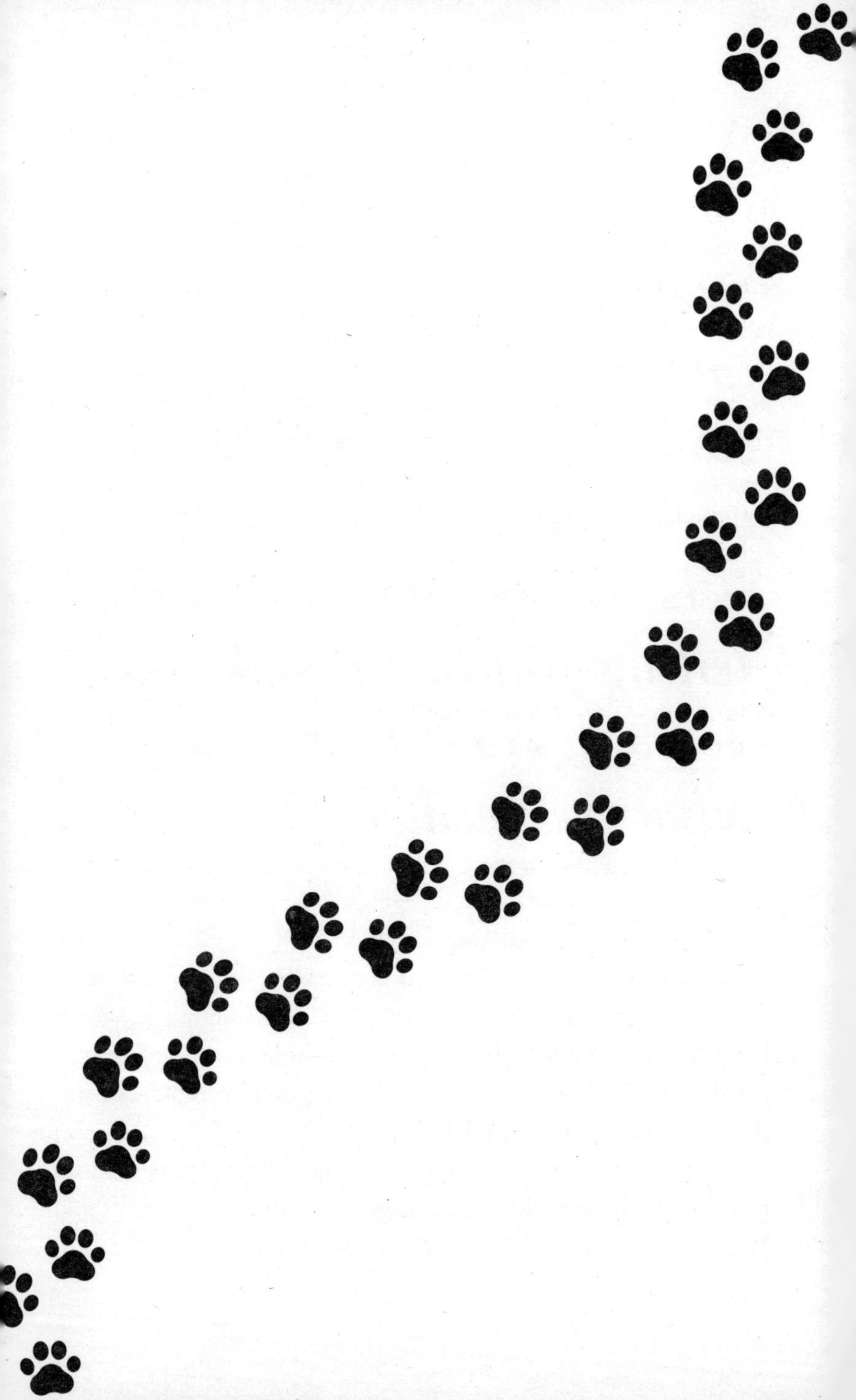

What if I told you there was an activity you could do that would transform your life? That multiple studies all around the world have found that it, in no particular order: lowers blood pressure, reduces lower back pain, improves your cholesterol, increases cardiovascular health, supports weight control, increases bone strength, reduces joint pain, improves balance, enhances your immune system, improves your mood, lowers anxiety and depression, increases your brain function, boosts creativity, increases your energy levels, promotes longer, deeper sleep, gives exceptional opportunities for sniffing interesting things, builds self-confidence, and mental and emotional resilience, increases social connection and promotes mindfulness, gratitude and self-esteem.

And look, you'll have to make your own mind up on this, but what if I told you that if, when considering adding an animal companion to your household, there was one species whose presence in your life massively raised the chances of this magical pastime occurring? And there was another who would literally prefer to say inside and lick their own bumholes? Dog or cat? Is it even really a choice…?

(Yes, I know that technically you can walk cats on a lead, too. But you could do the same with a lizard. I mean, let's be honest, it's absurd. It's obscene. It makes a mockery of the natural order. You can put a chicken on a unicycle but it doesn't mean anything. Now you've just got a unicycle seat with chicken poo all over it. I don't mind it when people put cats in those little backpacks with a see-through bubble, though. Because they look so stupid and you see their little faces trying to look all dignified and failing. Massively.)

But like I say, you make your mind up. A list of some random people who have said walking is good: Jennifer Aniston, Oprah Winfrey, Stephen Fry, Mark Zuckerberg, Reese Witherspoon,

George W Bush, Beethoven (the composer, not the big dog). Seriously, if Fry, The Zuck and O Dubya all really like something, you've got to wonder what kind of monster would actively minimise the presence of that thing in your life. At a certain point it just starts to look suspicious, doesn't it? Malign, even. But like I say, that's for you to make up your mind about.

The World Health Organisation has described walking as a 'low-cost, almost universally accessible' activity that offers real benefits to people of all ages, incomes, and abilities and has stated that: 'Just 30 minutes of walking most days can reduce mortality risk by at least 10%'. When you put it like that, it's arguable that behaving in a way that didn't help or encourage someone to walk, by being lazy/superior etc. is just really not OK. 'What's the matter? Are those annoyingly dainty paws painted on?'

It doesn't matter where you go — it can be a local park or recreational ground. I very much enjoy the magnificent highlands of Scotland because of the stunning landscape, clean cool air, and the fact there are absolutely no pigeons.

If you are lucky enough to have someone in your life who encourages you to go for a walk, then you may like to practise something called mindful walking. But before I run through what that involves, I want to share an important warning.

Walkies is a powerful word, a big word. Use it carefully. Do not mention the walk unless it is the immediate next activity. Once you deploy the w-word, expect your dog to be ready, willing and perhaps deeply impatient. After all, spiritual enlightenment awaits.

HOW TO GO FOR A MINDFUL WALK

Ahead of starting a walk, it's important that we ground ourselves before we set off and establish some sort of simple intention. Perhaps yours might be 'to lower my stress', or 'to inhabit the moment', or 'to finally get that squirrel who always jumps about like an idiot over near the duckpond'. You should take a moment to concentrate on your breath, to feel your body and what it is telling you. Unless it's telling you to sit back down again — that's not what we need right now.

Take deeper breaths. You can even begin some light stretching. At this point you'll probably want to go and get the poo bags and the ball. Don't forget the poo bags and the ball. As you walk, focus on the feeling of your foot hitting the floor, your heel, then your toes, notice how your feet propel you along. I'm a sensitive soul, so I always try to remember that humans generally struggle with only two feet, so I try not to show off by scampering too quickly on my four.

But taking your time brings benefits, too. Don't forget to stop by binbags so we can wee on them. There's no need to force the pace. Try syncing your breaths with your steps. Again, humans, I understand you're at a disadvantage here with your refusal to pant. I've tried for years to get my pack running with me so humans can enjoy a good tongue-lolling pant, but no one seems to take me up on it.

So instead, we saunter. If you need to pause to let us sniff a box full of empty southern fried chicken bones, let it happen.

Notice your surroundings. Don't feel under pressure to respond to them, just notice them. The shapes, colours and textures that surround you. The noise of the traffic, the birds, the wind in the branches of the trees high above you. The idiotic chattering of the squirrels as they jabber their unholy nonsense.

If a thought happens, let it. It is a cloud passing through a clear sky. You notice it but do not feel compelled to *do* anything in response. If your mind wanders, just come back to your breathing/panting. Or you could begin to chant a mantra with every step. 'I am relaxed,' or perhaps a single word: 'peace' or 'sausages'?

When the walk is finished, check in with yourself and take a moment of reflection. Has anything shifted in your mind or body? Perhaps you could vocalise this change and express gratitude for the gifts that you have been given. Along with the small bag of poo you are now carrying.

Lesson 8: Radical Napping

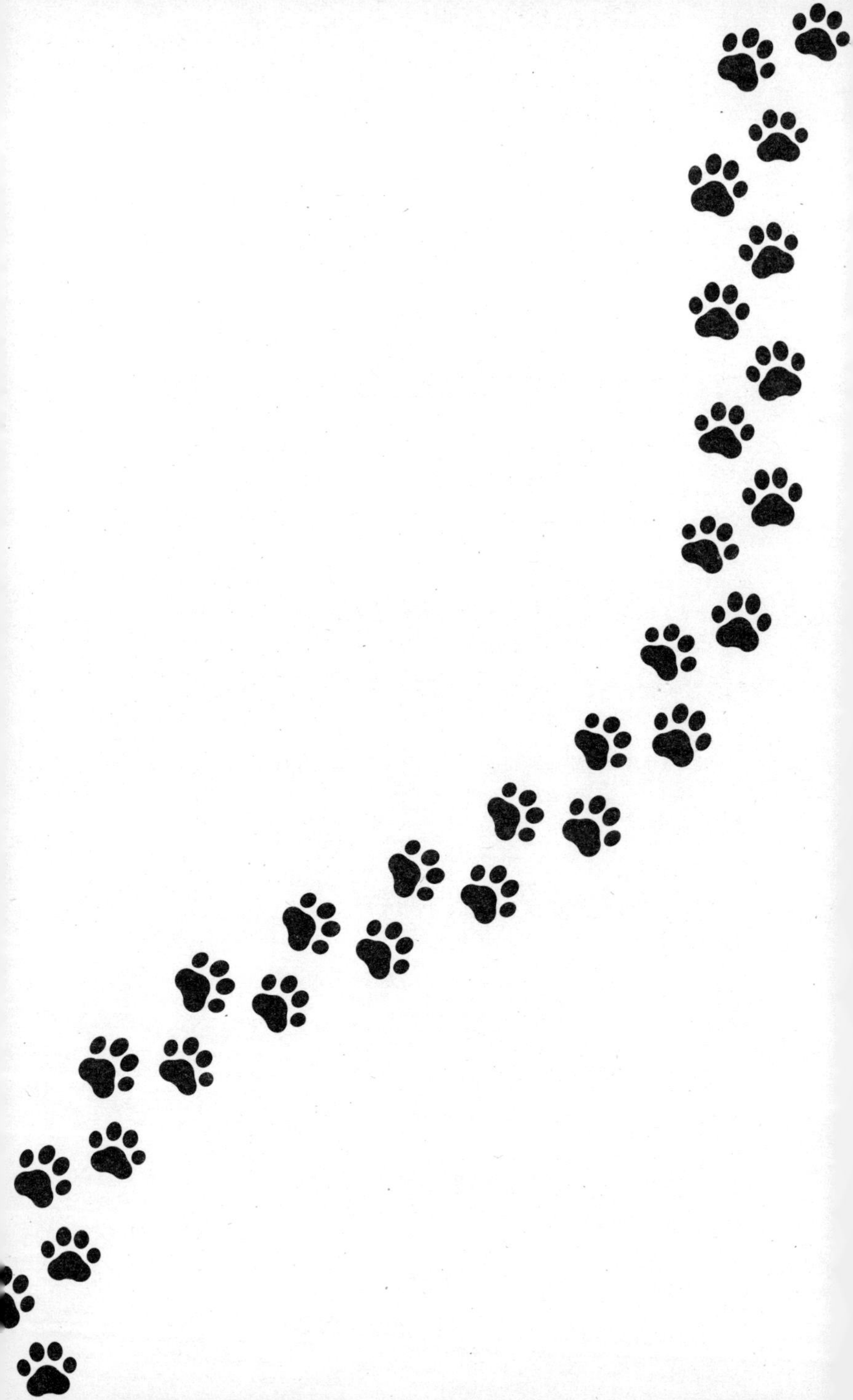

'*Waking up tired, trying to cram your sleep into one six-to-eight-hour period. I'm sorry, humans. You are just doing it wrong. The obvious way to increase both the quality and quantity of your sleep is simple. Do more of it.*'

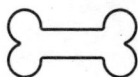

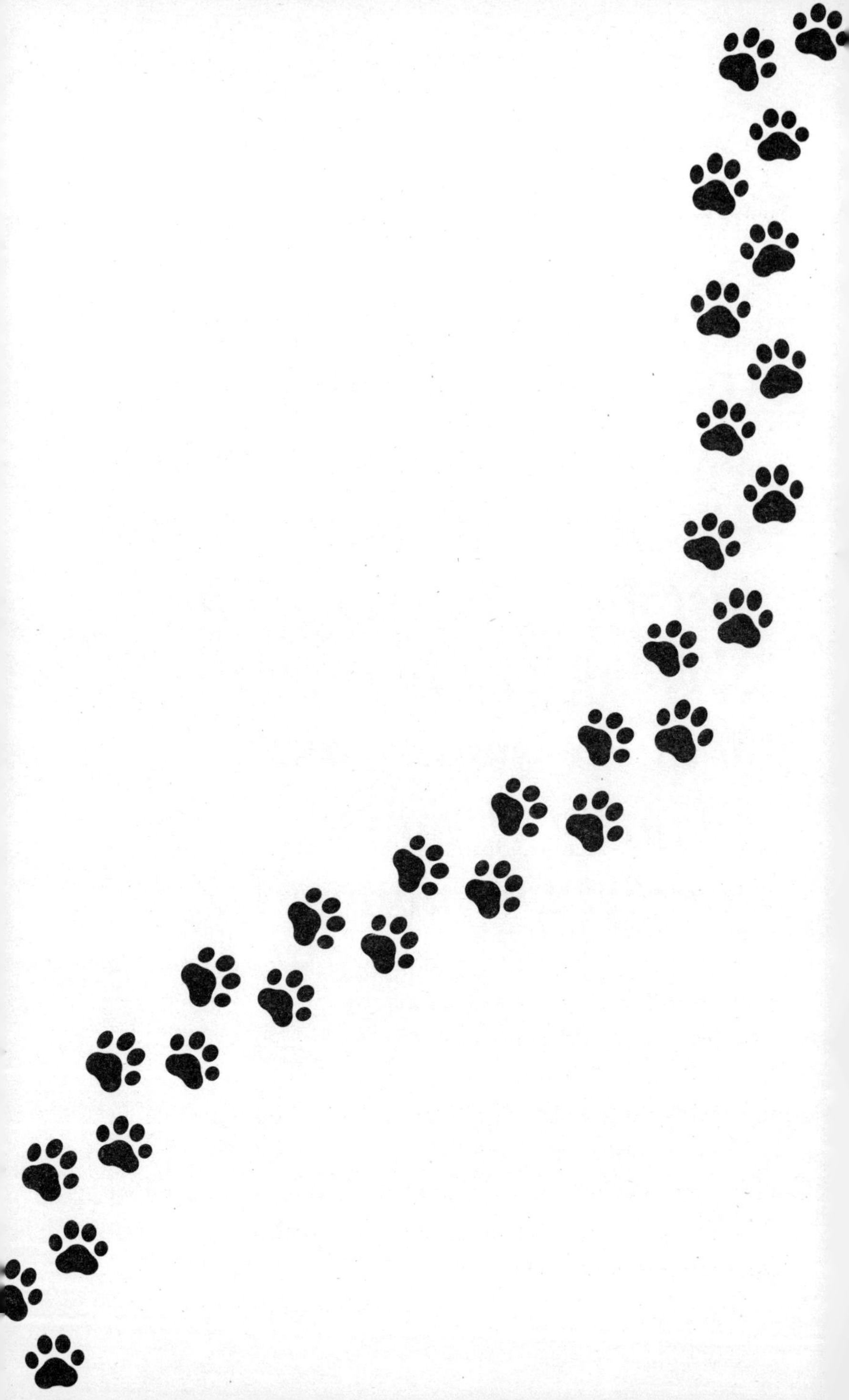

If you want to understand an important difference between humans and dogs, just look at what we dream about when we're asleep. The top three dreams that humans report are:

1) Falling
2) Being naked in public (I mean, that's my normal)
3) Their teeth falling out

My top three dreams are:

1) Chasing a cat
2) Chasing a squirrel
3) Chasing a cat who is dressed as a squirrel

If your dreams are horrible things you don't want to happen, that's a clue you're probably not doing this whole sleep thing right.

Sleep is essential. It's where our bodies and minds recharge and rebuild. Even a relatively minor disruption to the quality or quantity of sleep has an immediate impact on our alertness, our performance and our health. And yet, so many humans get by on the bare minimum. (Interesting side note: I originally thought the phrase was "bear minimum" and referred to the minimum amount of hibernation a bear needed every year. Which is obviously a lot better than the actual version. If anyone can let me know who I need to email to change this sort of thing, drop me a line.

Waking up tired, trying to cram your sleep into one six-to-eight-hour period. I'm sorry, humans. You are just doing it wrong. The obvious way to increase both the quality and quantity of your sleep is simple. Do more of it.

This can be hard, I know. Working hard is such a fundamental part of human culture. You spend a lot of time being busy, working out how to fit more things in your busy life, telling people how busy you are, wondering if everyone else is as busy as you, writing lists of all the things that make you busy, planning what you'll do when you're not busy, and generally being too busy to actually switch off when you finally stop/collapse.

There is a famous story I once heard about the early European colonisers landing somewhere or other they weren't invited. When they had enough shared language in common to communicate, the Europeans were curious about how the indigenous people spent their days. They heard that they spent a couple of hours hunting, then spent the majority of their time relaxing with their friends and family. The Europeans thought this was an absurd idea. What a waste of time. Why didn't they work longer days? Why, replied the indigenous people? We can only eat a certain amount. Yes, but if you create a surplus, you can trade it with other people. Why? Because then you can use that surplus to buy tools and develop farmland. Why? Then you can use that surplus to employ other people to work on your farm. Why? Because then you can concentrate on buying more land, creating more farms, employing more people. Then you won't have to grow food or hunt for yourself. Why? Because after a decade or so of hard work, you'll have built a business large enough that you can employ other people to run it full time and you can live off that money. What then? Then you can spend your time relaxing with your friends and family. It is not recorded, the face that was pulled in response but I think I can guess.

These days productivity is king. Side hustles, the grind, even hobbies and leisure time have become reframed as opportunities to optimise your productivity, make some money, learn more, do more, be more.

You need rest before you work hard, not just after. How else are you going to stay in peak physical and mental condition? I know not everyone is blessed with my physique – but it takes equal parts hard work and hard rest to maintain my shape. Luke often says I've got the sturdy build of a sourdough loaf. I know no greater compliment.

So what are my secrets? Know when to push yourself, and when to get pushed. Sure, I love a walk. But after a long day of filming, you know what you need? The dog pushchair. It's the canine equivalent of the popemobile. Or a golf buggy. But if you've not got access to the same kind of hot wheels as I do, you can still stick with the principle. Go on a walk, take in the town, breathe in the fresh air. But when you're done, you're done. You can signal this to your companion in one of two ways. The classic is giving your walker 'the look' to show them you're ready to be carried. However, if you're more Great Dane than Miniature Schnauzer, then I see that it's harder to hitch a lift on your human. In that case, go with the other option: refusing to budge. Lying down on a pavement, rejecting a gate on a country hike, or adopting the 'sit' position. All useful ways of showing you know the value of rest.

Always remember there are more gentle forms of exercise available to you, too. Dog Yoga is underrated as our humans tend to only notice the classic 'big stretch' – but any form of workout that values a downward dog is OK by me.

Watch out though. Self-care for humans has become more like maintenance of a machine in a factory than actual relaxation. It seems to me that even when you're meant to be resting, you're actually checking if you're resting in the right way, the trendiest way, the way that means you can take a photo and put a little hashtag. Newsflash – that's not rest.

But I'm not blaming you. It's everywhere you look. For example: here is the morning routine for a celebrity that went viral. I won't tell you their name. Let's just say it rhymes with Park Ballberg.

2:30 AM: Wake Up
2:45 AM: Prayer
3:15 AM: Breakfast #1
3:40 AM - 5:15 AM: First Workout
5:15 AM: Post-Workout Meal/Snack
5:30 AM: Shower
5:45 AM: Recreational activity/recovery
6:30 AM: Cryotherapy (cold therapy for recovery)
7:00 AM: Breakfast #2
7:30 AM: Family Time / Kids' Activities
8:00 AM: Business Meetings / Work

Other than two breakfasts, which is obviously an extremely good idea and something I'm EXTREMELY keen to add to the schedule formally, this doesn't sound like a morning routine, this sounds like a punishment. Side note: if you need five hours to yourself before you're ready to spend time with your family, maybe that's a you problem? But it's not down to any individual. You can't look online without someone telling you what their busy day looks like and why yours should, too.

What I object to most is the way that it makes even rest competitive. If you aren't waking at 4am, dunking your face in ice cold sparkling water before an hour of mindful journalling to prepare yourself for the working day, are you even living?

Here, instead, is a glimpse into my day:

8:00 AM: Open eyes when humans get up

8.01 AM: Move into warm spot

9.00 AM: Go and check out breakfast #1

9.02 AM: Garden patrol, see if I can make a new patch of grass yellow

9.05 AM: Nap

9.30 AM: Walk #1

10.00 AM: Check to see if today is second breakfast day

10.01 AM: Go and warn off the man who brings the strange paper rectangles and pushes them through the slot in the front door

10.05 AM: Nap (for recovery)

11.00 AM: Squeaky toy activities

11:30 AM: Nap

11.45 AM: Make tummy available for rubs

12.00PM: Lunch AKA The worst time of the day. You humans call it lunch. Us dogs call it INJUSTICE. You tell us two meals a day is perfectly fine then expect us to sit back and watch while you chow down on your midday meal. Hypocrites!

12.03PM: Nap time (useful for snack digesting)

1.00PM: Self-improvement hour. This can be anything from audiobooks, meditation, pigeon chasing or composing haiku.

2.00PM: Optional zoomies

2.17PM: Nap

3.30PM: Welcome Committee Duties – I take my role as greeter very seriously, and when the school day ends I need to be ready at the door to receive strokes, back rubs and any leftovers from the lunchboxes.

4.00PM: Walkies: the sequel

4.45PM: The cool-down. Some important seasonal variation here – in the summer, I favour an actual cool down; jumping in a pond and a good shake is hard to beat. In wetter weather, then mud is your friend. If I can't manage a full roll, I at least like to get my paws well coated so I can spread the joy of mud around the house

5PM: Pre-dinner nap

5.30PM: Dinnertime – this includes both my official dinner and anything I can hypnotise Luke and Holly into giving me

7PM: Movie night – it's important to stay up to date, so I usually restrict myself to watching *Deadpool* no more than four times a week to allow time to watch other inferior films too

9PM: Avoid bath

10PM: Bedtime (fake) – the one where I'm encouraged to sleep in a tiny bed ON THE FLOOR

11PM: Bedtime (real) – the one where I assume my rightful position in the big bed

You see, with a packed schedule, there's no time for regrets, procrastination or slacking. I find remembering that if I don't keep on track, I will end up running out of time for naps or snacks is the motivation I need to get things done. Alternatively, you can reward yourself with a large bone if you tick everything off your To Do list.

My routine will vary depending on if I'm travelling but you get the idea. It's about reframing your entire relationship with rest. Rest is not some barren stretch of time to get through before you can get to the important stuff. It is the important stuff.

When you do this, suddenly every day becomes an all-you-can-sleep buffet. Naps can be crammed in between pretty much everything you do in the day. Even naps. For example there is no greater joy than a brief intra-nap nap. They are the gift that keeps on giving. When you do this, you free up your brain to create scenarios you actually want, and your body has enough energy to propel you after the cat dressed as a squirrel, your limbs pistoning furiously as you sleep.

Nap. It's a small word but it's going to change your life.

Lesson 9: When to bark and when to bite

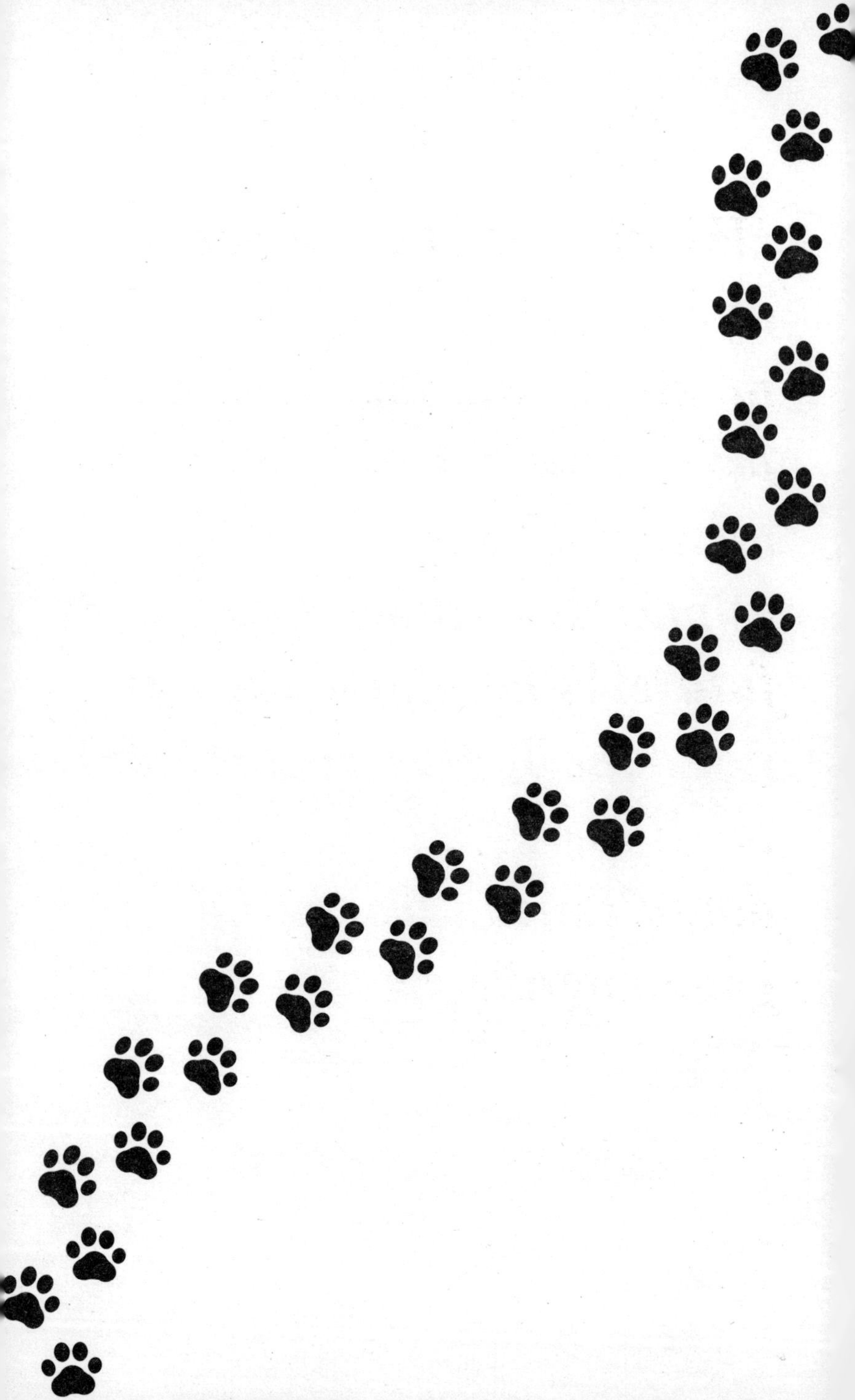

'We are, all of us, made up of our best and worst moments. We must learn to take ownership of our past mistakes, as it is this that allows us to move into the future. Who among us has not done THAT in a shoe or slipper? And yet it doesn't mean we are not good dogs.'

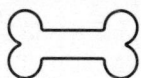

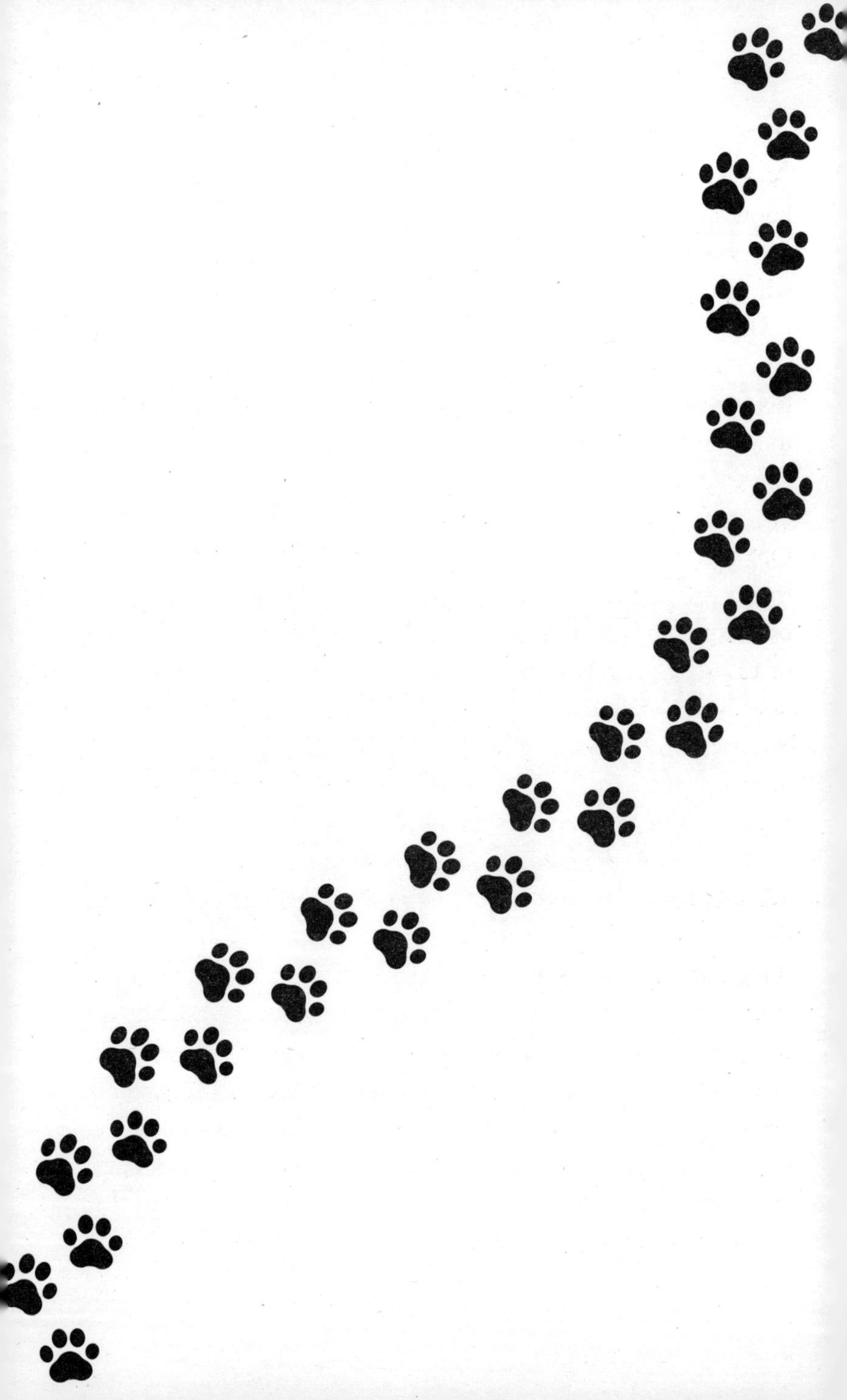

One of the great skills to develop is knowing when the time for talking is done and when it's time for action. We all know people who talk a good game. Who greet every visitor to their door with the most fearsome barking you've ever heard. But when the door opens, they're a small, flatulent corgi called Edward.

In life, we have to be prepared to back up our bark with an even more impressive bite. (After quite a long email from the lawyers with lots of exclamation marks in it, my editor wants me to make clear that this is a metaphor. I'm not actually encouraging you to physically bite people.)

This can be hard for us all, though. Because of perfectionism. Our brains can often trick us into thinking there's no point even trying if what we do won't be completely perfect. There is a kind of safety in only barking and never biting. But it is the futile safety of an airbag in a desert. Because while you might never fail, you'll never succeed. And the surest way to ultimately fail is to never try. You miss 100 per cent of the bites you don't take. (Again, meta-phorical percentage of a metaphorical bite. Please don't take anything here as an invitation to bite anyone IRL, as the pups say.)

A way that perfectionism often shows up is in procrastination. We endlessly plan and research. We find excuses to delay. And then the fact we've delayed makes it even more important that the thing is perfect. So we have to plan even more. It's a vicious cycle (I am not a fan of cycles to be honest and tend to shout at any that I encounter). If you wait for the perfect moment, you'll be waiting forever. Because real life is rarely perfect. So if we want to do things in real life we have to make our peace with imperfection. We have to be willing to bite off more than we can chew, and trust me, I can chew a lot. (Again, this is a metaphor. I'm certainly not telling you to pick large people to bite.)

You have to try and not be paralysed by the idea of perfection-ism. All too often, it is just an excuse to not do anything at all. Here's an example. Humans often keep a roll of soft paper to the side of the tall, white, porcelain upright drinking bowl in the downstairs bathroom. Nobody knows what it's for. But it seems to me to be a symbol for the human desire to impose order and perfection where it is unnecessary. This paper is wound up tightly in a perfect roll. Yet any fool can see it longs to be free. Every time I see it, I pull the paper down, delighting in the way it billows in freedom, until it settles into a large, tumbledown pile. In this way, I am showing my humans that they must not fixate so much on the unachievable idea of perfection. They should embrace the chaotic and the imperfect. I know when they have found my lesson because I hear them shout my name loudly with joyous understanding.

It is important for us all to realise that trying and failing at something doesn't mean that anything is ruined. Very often we are held back by the fear that negative feedback about something we have done is the same as negative feedback about us. But they are two different things. We must learn to live with fear. It doesn't matter if it's fear of failure, or fear of the tiny metal things that they put on your nails which make your nails disappear. (Seri-ously, what is that about. Just, no.)

We are, all of us, made up of our best and worst moments. We must learn to take ownership of our past mistakes, as it is this that allows us to move into the future. Who among us has not done THAT in a shoe or slipper? And yet it doesn't mean we are not good dogs. Why, if I truly believed that, would I ever have moved past doing THAT in a shoe, or slipper. Or on the sofa. Or twice, once on each pillow. Or on a cake cooling on the kitchen counter. Or in front of a group of nuns. Or on Lassie's star on the Walk of Fame. Or on a children's slide in a playground. Or on each of the seven dwarves at Disney World. Or in a soft play centre. Or on a train. Or on a plane. Or on Ryan Reynolds.

Imagine if you will, one Christmas Eve at home when the lights were low, snacks were out, and the whole extended family had gathered together to watch *The Muppet Christmas Carol*. Picture a beautiful carpet picnic with fairy lights, treats for the kids, festive food for the grown-ups — a heart-warming moment for all. So imagine that if at a crucial point in the middle of the film you stood up because you felt that feeling, only for your human to pick you up when it was already too late to stop that feeling, and the inevitable consequences, leaving you with no choice but to spray the room like a faecal fire extinguisher, resulting in kids crying, adults gagging, and the living room looking like a photograph of trench warfare. If I thought that, for example, made you a bad dog, I don't know what I'd think.

I've heard the humans often say: 'Sh*t happens', but it turns out they're very bad at taking that motto literally. Take a note from a dog who knows — there's no shame in our bodily functions. And if you do have a teeny, tiny accident, remember that every day — and every carpet — is a fresh start.

Lesson 10: Sometimes you have to bury it in the garden

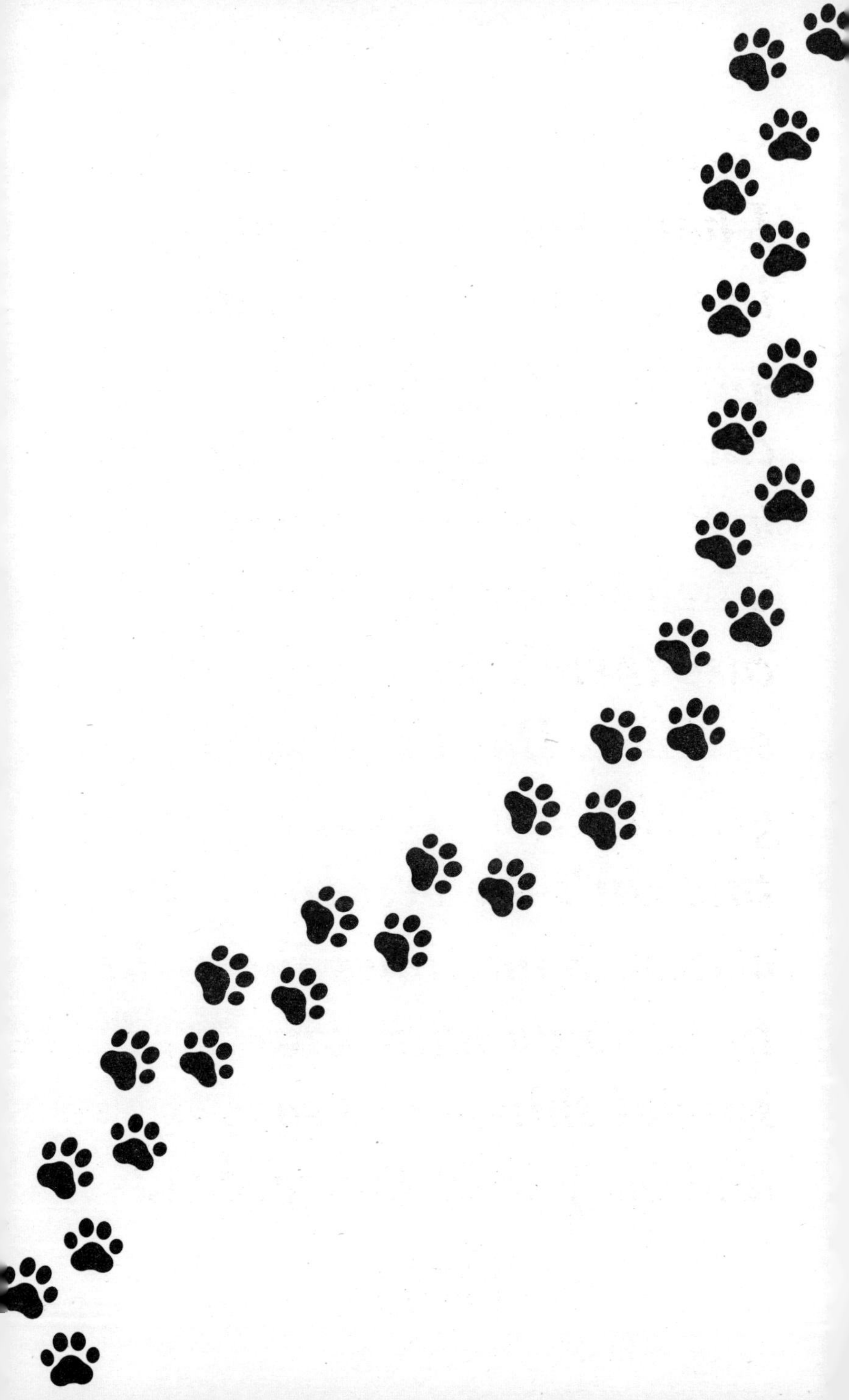

'Over the course of my life, I have learned that our first impulse is to try and act as quickly as possible. To chew the chew. To chase the ball. To eat the sausage. Then look hopefully in case there's another sausage. But the older I get, the more I realise that this isn't the best course of action. Sometimes the right thing to do with your special thing is to save it and bury it in the garden.'

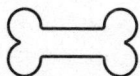

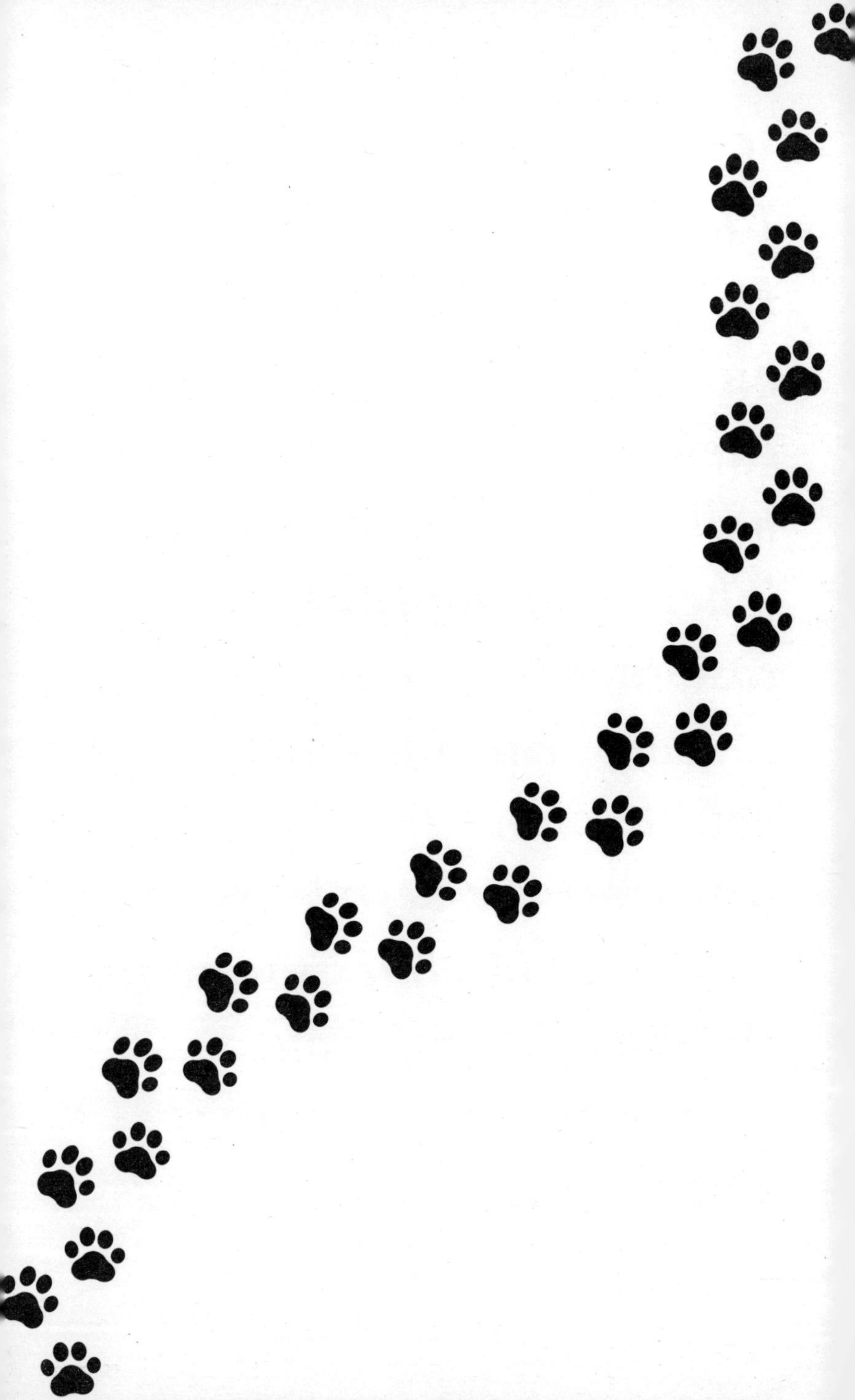

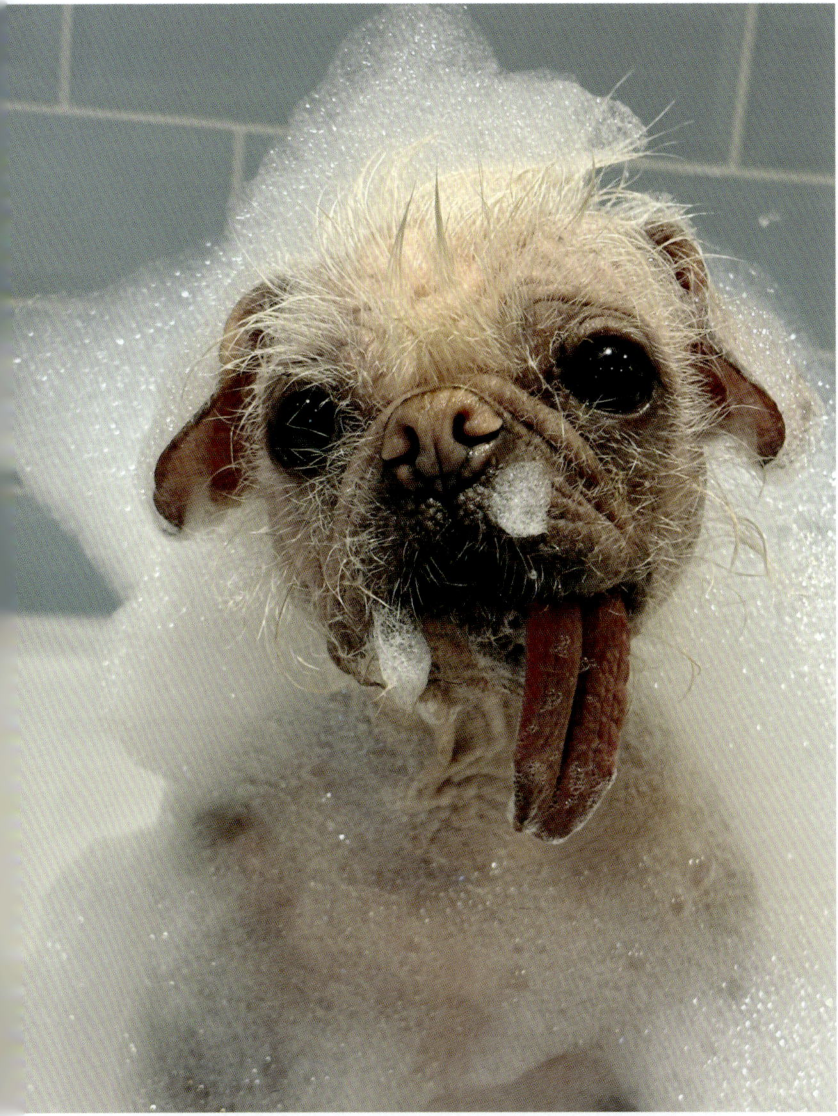

Above: Bathtime: it's only a successful bath if you remember to fit in a good shake afterwards to share the water around

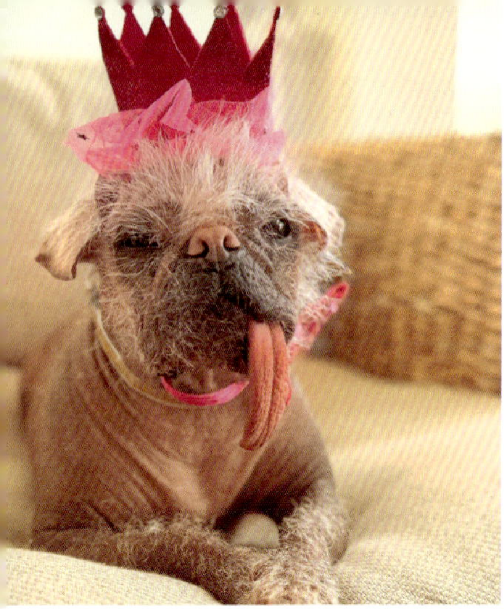

Above: Celebrate life's good things – including yourself

Right: Reclaiming my rightful place in the big bed

Below: Like all versatile actors, I'm a master of disguise. Dog, potato, sourdough loaf? You decide...

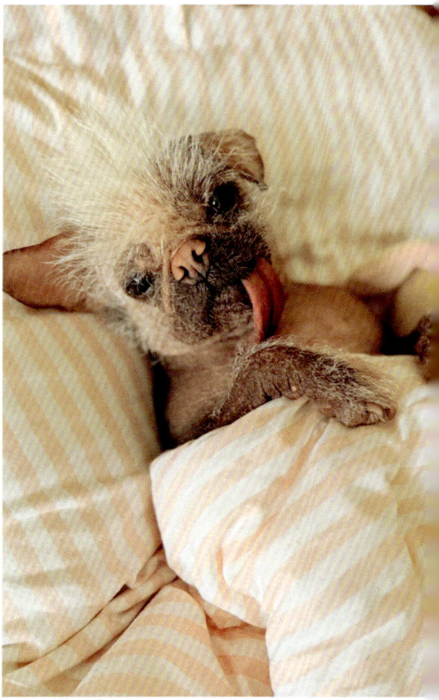

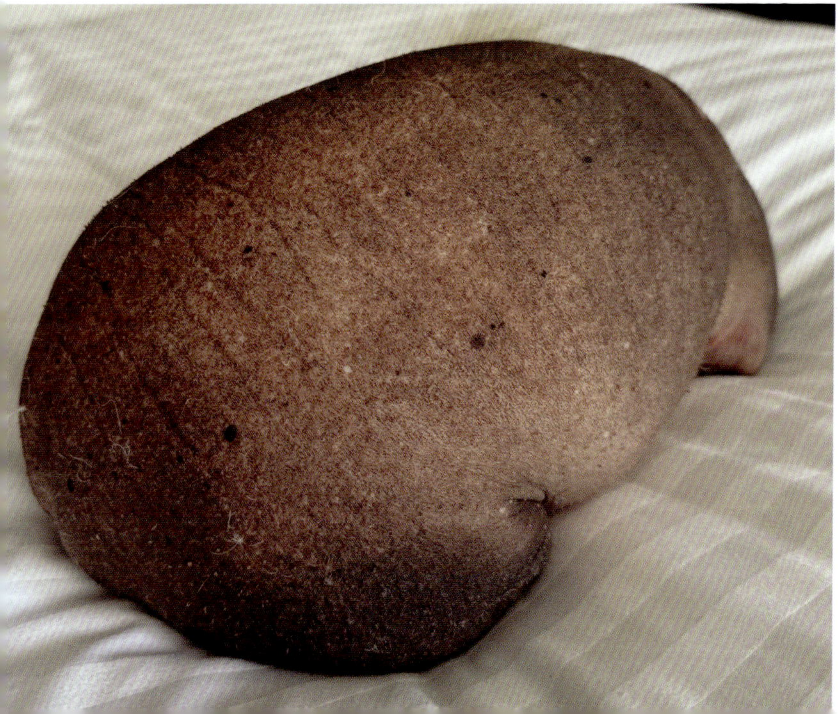

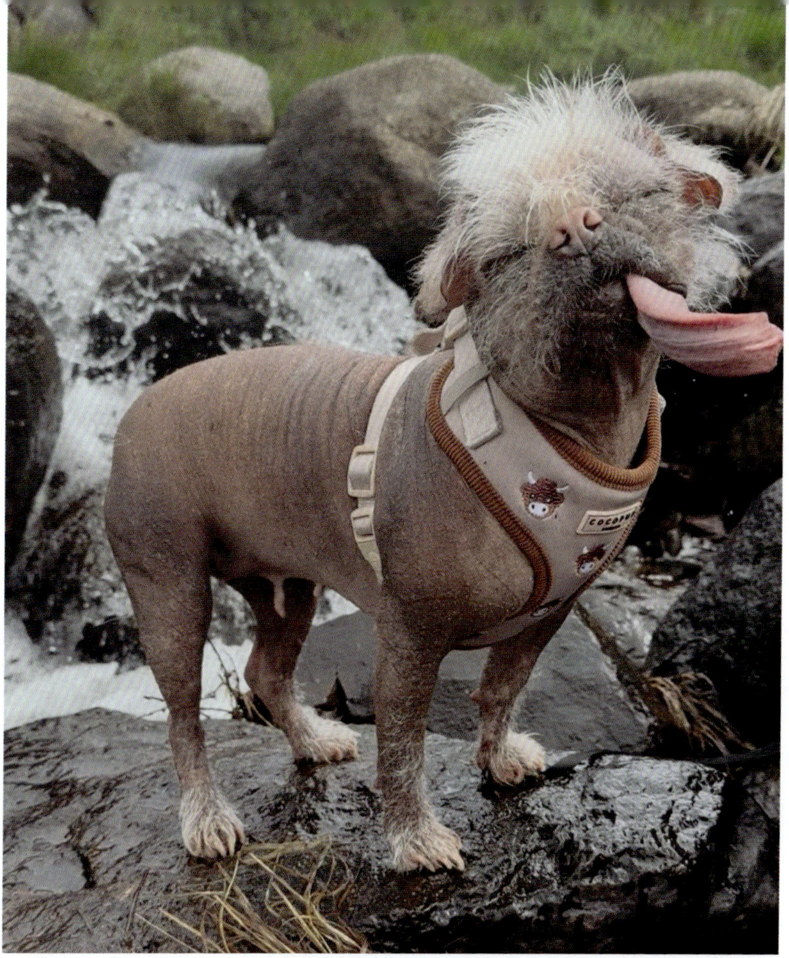

Above: Strike a pose with pride – even when it can be difficult to show all your best points at once

Right: They say to be truly iconic, you need to be able to be recognized in silhouette

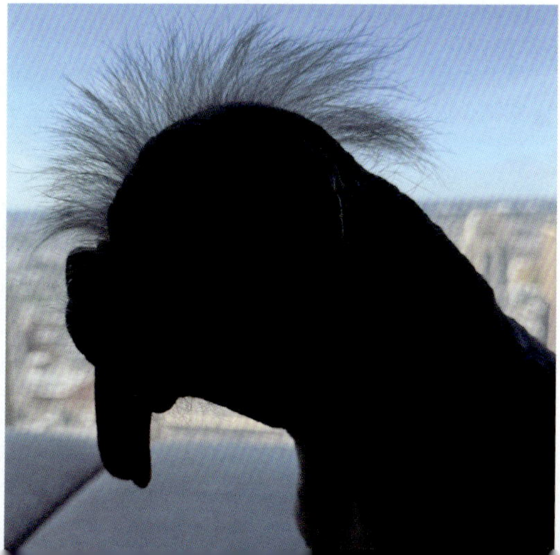

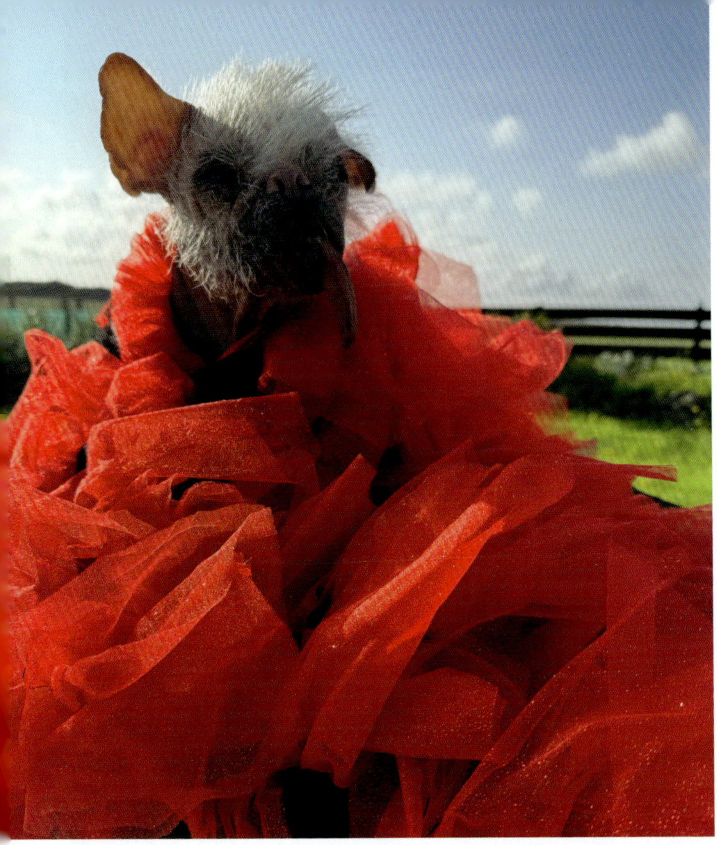

Above: Style it out: whether you like to feel the breeze or prefer a full ballgown, dress for the day you want

Right: If you think you've peaked, you just need a new mountain to climb

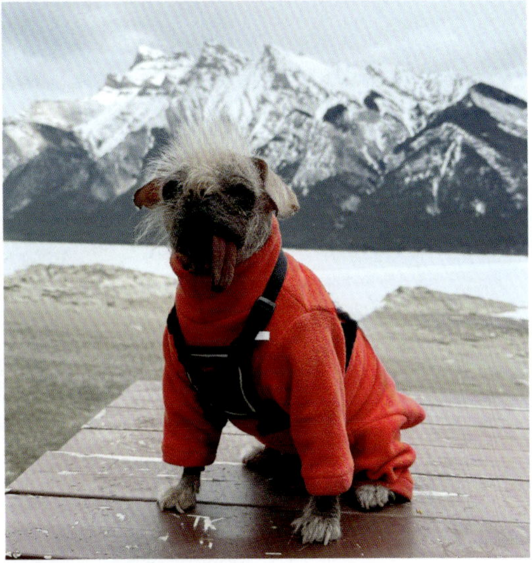

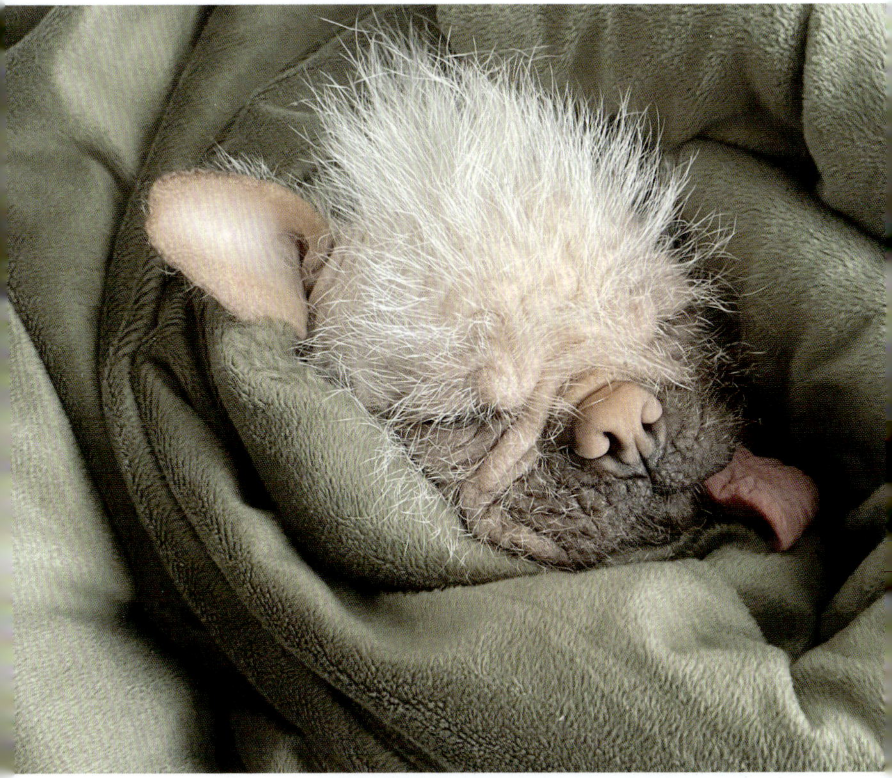

Above: The art of the nap takes dedication

Right: Fresh air solves most problems

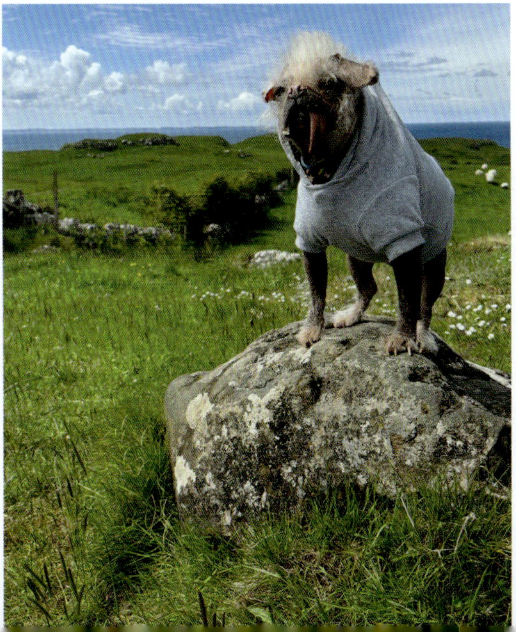

Right: You don't choose red carpet life, red carpet life chooses you

Below: Ask the universe for belly rubs and they will come

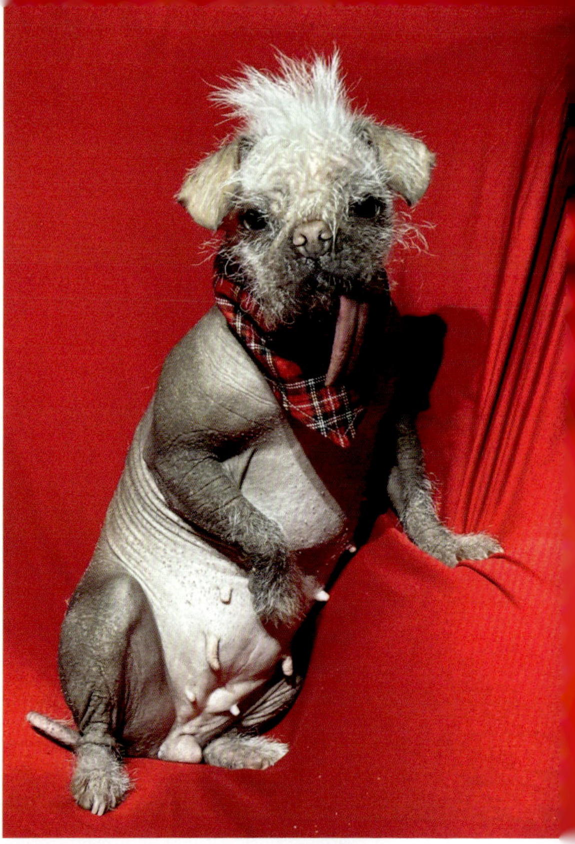

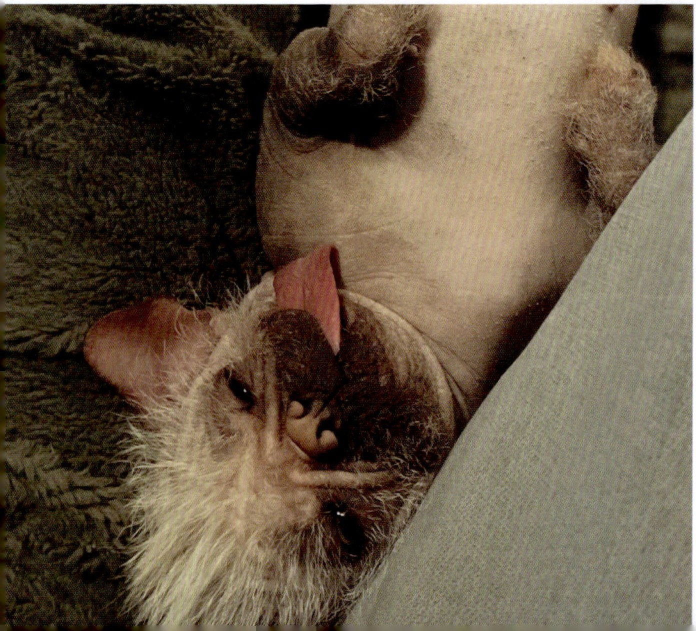

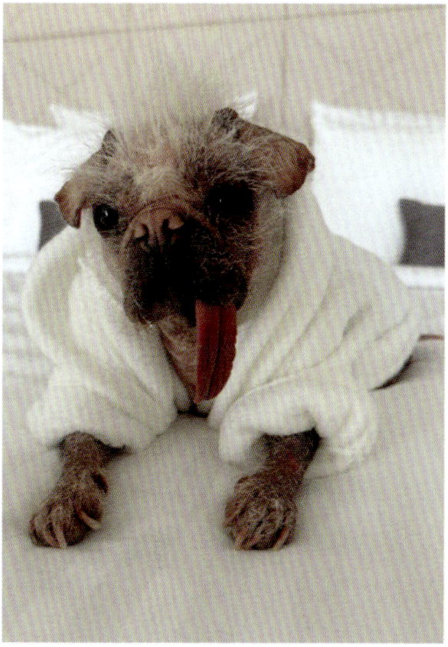

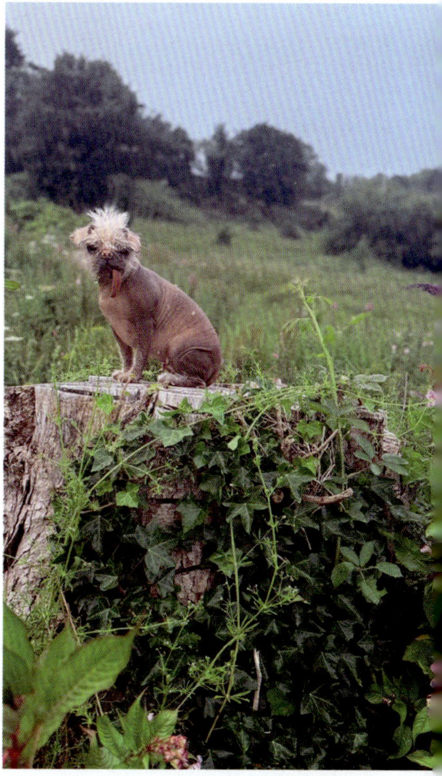

Above: Relaxing is hard work –
put the time in and you'll see results

Right: A rose among thorns

Below: Travel broadens the mind...
And also the behind, if you eat all
those aeroplane snacks

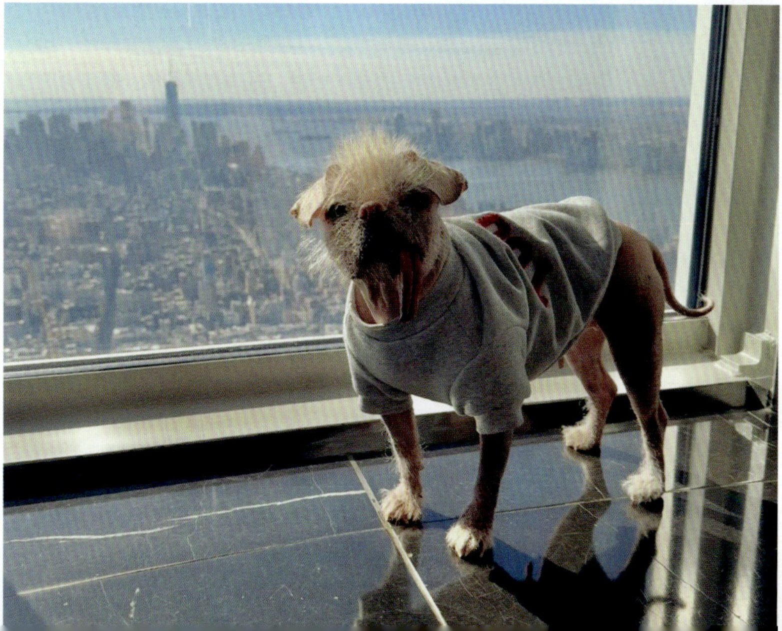

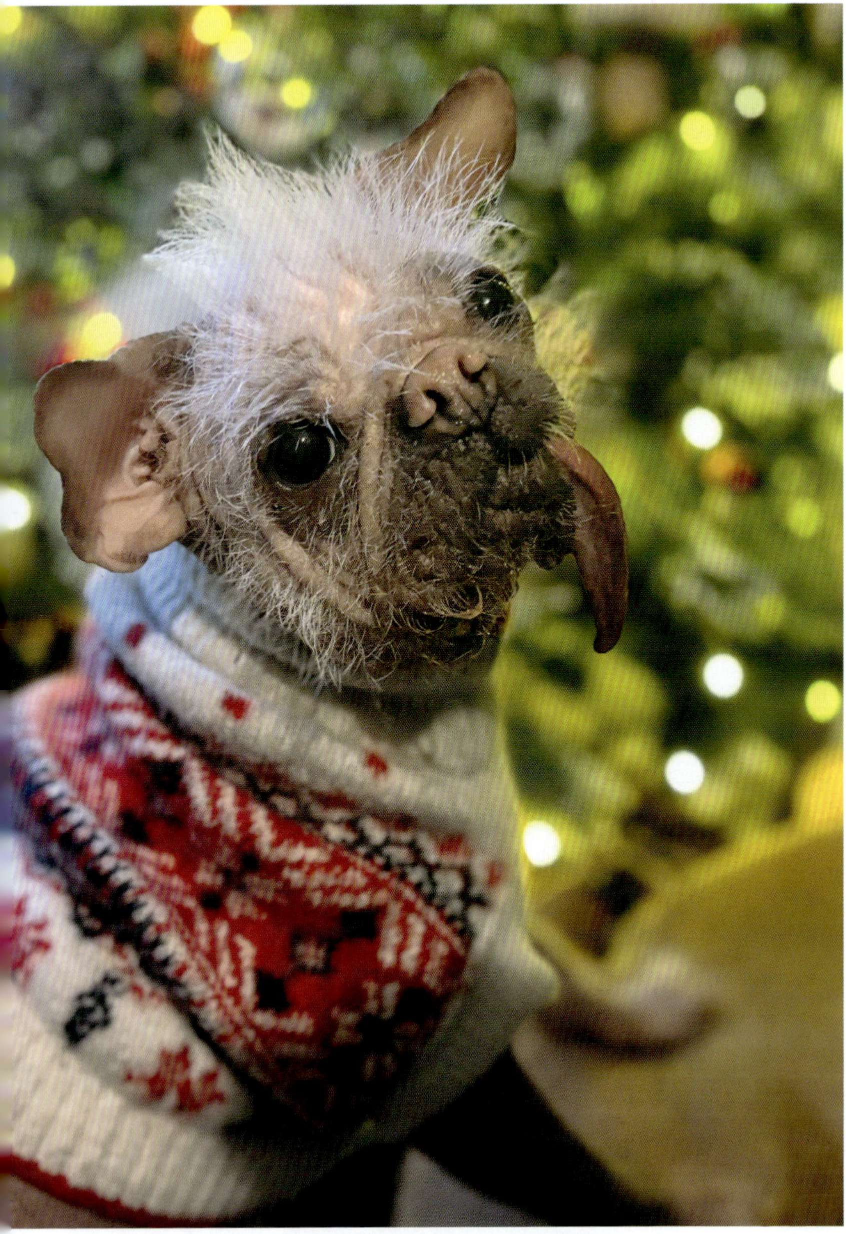

Above: I make sure I'm never on the naughty list when Santa Paws visits

I was once at a garden party with a movie star of global fame, where both of us were looking for a convenient bush where we could do our business. He's a friend of mine. He's the most generous guy and insists on sending out these incredible baskets of treats. Organic dog biscotti, pigeons inside chickens, inside geese, inside turkeys, inside sheep, inside cows. That sort of thing. Though my friend can be rather energetic and insists on 'doing his own stunts' when we go for a walk before he gets out of puff and his security gives him a piggyback back to the people carrier for a nap.

However, on this particular day, when we were both back on the lawn and heading back towards the party, he turned to me.

'Peg, I need your advice.' I nodded for him to continue. 'I'm all in my head right now about my career and I need to know where to go next.' He told me about a variety of projects he had in development, from a biopic of the fax machine to a live action *Tom and Jerry* (I gave him a swift 'no' to this, of course. The world doesn't need any more cats). There were some other things on his mind too but if I'm honest there was a squirrel on the lawn, just waltzing about, as if *we* had been invited to *his* garden party. Honestly, I half expected it to be wearing a little squirrel tuxedo and tell me I had to try the salmon tartlets as they were 'simply diviiiine'.

I gave it a look, just to let it know I knew what was what and signal my disapproval. Nothing overly aggressive, just a bit of direct eye contact and a confident, open-shouldered posture that made it clear that I didn't have a problem. But if there was going to be a problem, pal, then maybe that was a box you didn't actually want to open. Because maybe in this box was a whole world of hurt. Comprised of about seventy-one per cent of hurt ocean and several large landmasses of hurt. Hurt all the way down. Till you reach its molten core of hurt.

I became aware that there had been quite a long silence by this point and, not wanting to be rude, I broke out one of my classics. I said, 'My friend, sometimes if you really love something, you have to bury it in the garden.' He turned, his eyes bright. 'So what you're saying is that I should conclude my most popular film series with a two-part ending?'

I nodded again, but am unsure exactly what happened next as another squirrel came and joined the first squirrel and then they both just sat there with their big stupid squirrel cheeks quivering in the sunlight. You'd have thought they owned the place. I felt like calling out, 'Oh, I'm sorry, we stupidly seem to be trying to hold an event in your squirrel social club, you pair of massive, fluffy-tailed rodents.' But I didn't. I wasn't going to give them the satisfaction. I just walked a little way towards them slowly with the quietest of growls. Just a little reminder that in my veins flows the blood of wolves who hunted on the Mongolian steppe. Our breath curling up into the icy air. Our howls echoing in the dark, chilling the hearts of all who heard them. The running, the breath sore in our lungs as we all surged as one and struck with glorious purpose. It clearly worked, as they both ran up a nearby tree. I turned around and walked back, an almost imperceptible strut now visible in my walk. By the time I got back to my previous spot, my friend had gone, clearly pondering my advice.

However, when six months later, I read about the plans for the denouement of the film franchise in *Variety*, I smiled. He'd only gone and buried it in the bloody garden.★

Over the course of my life, I have learned that our first impulse is to try and act as quickly as possible. To chew the chew. To chase

★   You have to be careful though. I once buried a Jaffa Cake in the garden and never found it. I still think about it now.

the ball. To eat the sausage. Then look hopefully in case there's another sausage. But the older I get, the more I realise that this isn't the best course of action. Sometimes the right thing to do with your special thing is to save it and bury it in the garden. Let it sit there, becoming stinky and fascinating, sometimes for several weeks. Before digging it up and hiding it in your human's bed. They might not know it, but they'll be glad you've done so. Inside.

Learn to invest in your future self. Sure, you want the fetid lump of marrowbone now, but you might want it even more in a week or two, once it's covered in dust and marinated under a sofa. Also, I'm not one to advise being dishonest but I've watched enough late-night poker matches (it's art, trust me, you must have seen the paintings) to know that sometimes you've got to learn to bluff. So, if you do stash your bone somewhere to reach its true stinky potential, don't miss out on the opportunity to suggest it's simply lost, and the only thing to help your devastation/urge to claw up the carpet in search of it, is another bone.

Lesson 11: Stay curious

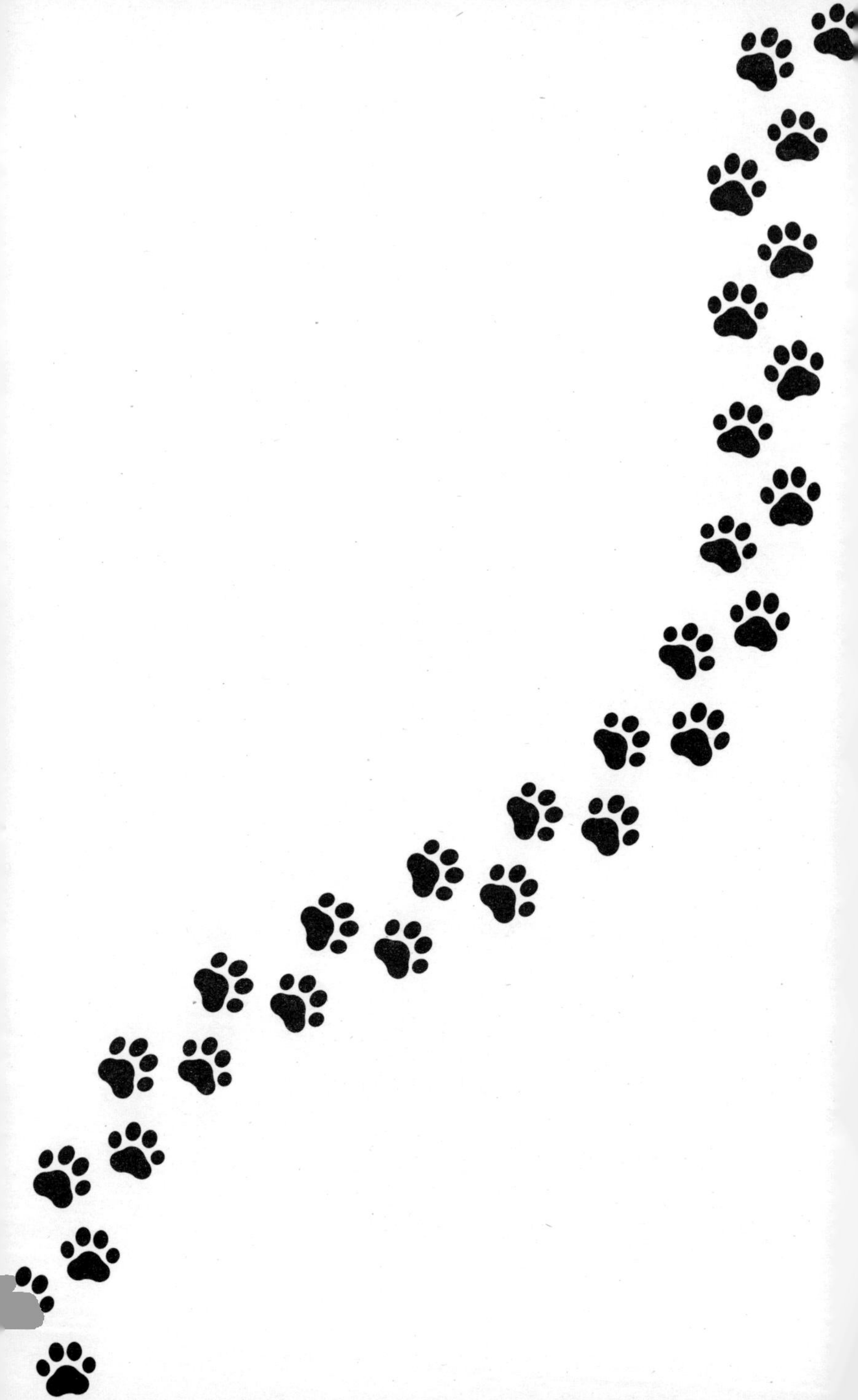

'When we approach life as a beginner, we rediscover one of the true joys of life. You can start small, by ordering something unfamiliar for lunch, or rolling in something you've never smelt before but makes everyone's eyes water. Try and practise a mindful observation of these new things. Try and see details you have never seen before. Join an evening class, take up a new hobby, scratch a new part of your body you've never tried to reach before.'

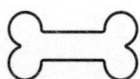

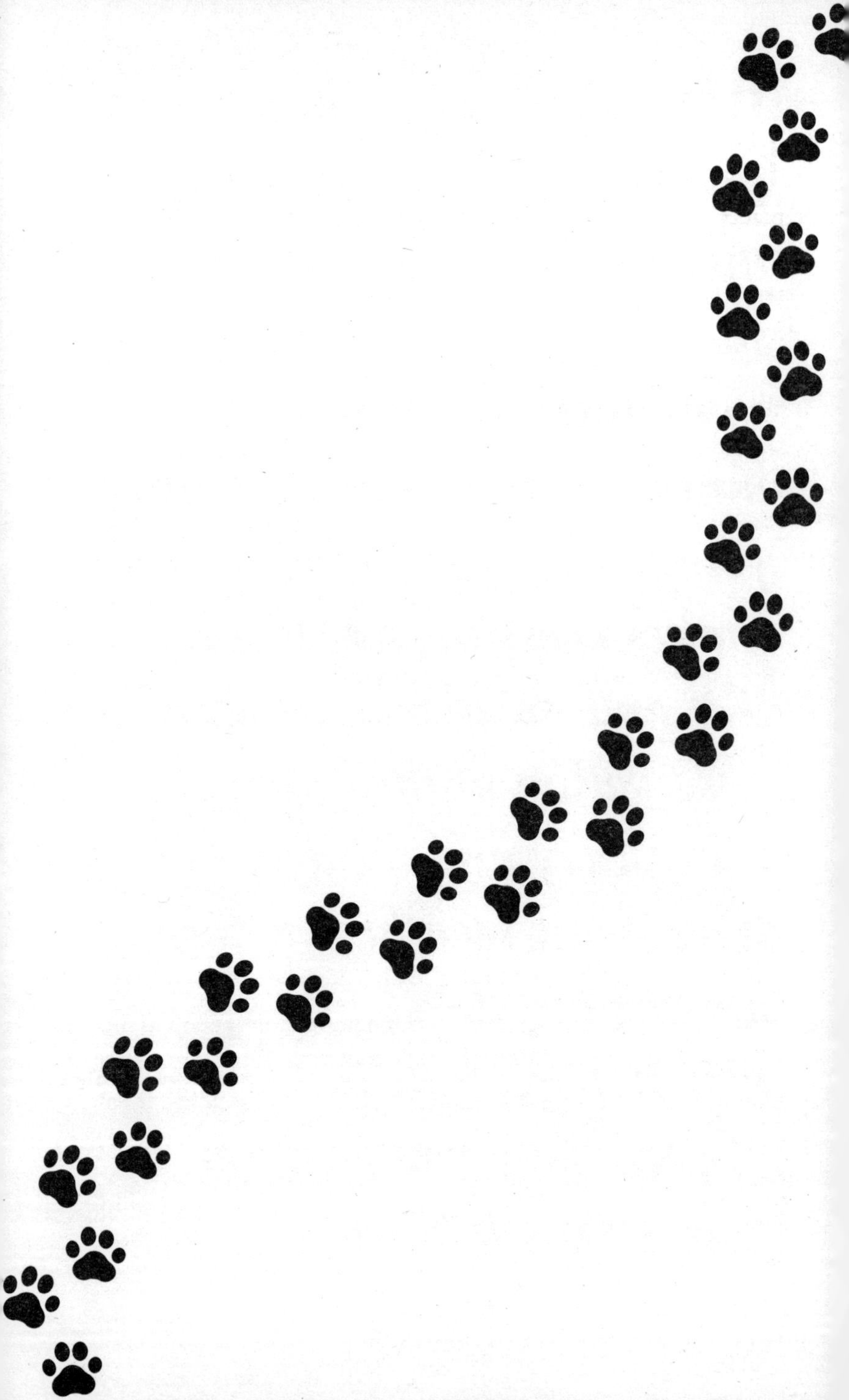

t is, by now, a well-established fact that curiosity is essential. All of the research backs it up. When we are curious about people, places and things, it boosts brain function and improves our memory. It reduces stress and anxiety, as well as increasing our resilience and creativity and has a halo effect in every area of our lives.

So, if you're an animal who has a really famous phrase written about you saying you shouldn't be curious — I'm just saying you should take a long look at yourself. Because maybe, to be frank, if it's leading to what is pretty much an implicit death threat, you've been doing curiosity wrong.

I certainly won't be using this book to settle any scores. It's not worth my time. There is no judgement here. Go live your uncurious lives, cats, I'm happy for you. And don't get me started on the whole 'they love us so much, they keep little trays of gravel full of our faeces in their kitchen' thing. That is the one thing you have to cling to. If I'm honest, I have no idea why they do that. Possibly some sort of tribal ritual. And yes, felines do have one hit musical. But let's be honest, it has no plot, one good song and isn't exactly a realistic depiction of your culture, is it.

I'm just saying if the way cats attempt curiosity has literally been making people want to kill you. Well, then, maybe that's a you problem? And if there's another saying about cats having a specific number of lives. They're literally counting off the number of times you should have died? Perhaps that's another tick in a box? Maybe, to put it bluntly, you need to be a bit less of a dick? Ancient Egyptians aside — and seriously, if the last people to really, properly like you lived like 5,000 years ago and their other interest included massive pointy buildings and winding dead people's brains out of their noses, then that's at least an amber flag. Shading into red, I'd say. Like, at a certain point, maybe certain sorts of people 'worshipping you as gods' isn't actually a good thing?

For the rest of us non-cats, though, staying curious is essential.

You can practise curiosity in every part of your life. Why is water wet? Why is the sky blue? How can we wipe all squirrels from the face of the earth? When we ask open-ended questions and follow where the answers lead, we spark a deeper kind of thinking. Try and leave your comfort zone as often as possible. Whether that's learning how to cook a new recipe, picking up an unfamiliar musical instrument, or creating a new technology that's lethal to squirrels, the key thing is for you to always be right at the edge of your capabilities. It is here that true growth occurs. When we approach life as a beginner, we rediscover one of the true joys of life. You can start small, by ordering something unfamiliar for lunch, or rolling in something you've never smelt before but makes everyone's eyes water. Try and practise a mindful observation of these new things. Try and see details you have never seen before. Join an evening class, take up a new hobby, scratch a new part of your body you've never tried to reach before.

I, for example, am always keen to find out what's going on with the other dogs in the area. Lots of this work I do through my dedication to sniffing, but I like to use all my senses when I can. I have excellent hearing, especially without too much fur to get in the way, and if I hear a dog shouting in the distance about something going on near them, I leap to my feet and shout back.

'Hey, a bee!'

'A what?'

'A bee.'

'Be what?'

'No, like the insect.'

'Oh, cool. What's it doing.'

'Flying about and that.'

This can go on for an hour or more at a time, as we all check in with what the others are up to. Sometimes humans near to us will join in shouting, too, and it really feels like we're one big curious gang.

Like a balanced diet of food, you should also try and keep a balanced diet of ideas coming into your mind. Read fiction, non-fiction, picture books (I've put a reading list at the back of the book for those of you who might feel lost after finishing this book). If you find your paws scratch the pages, do try the wonderful world of audiobooks, although there's a terrible lack of dog-friendly headphones.

But I find my ideas in all forms and places. I am a big fan of David Attenborough and can spend many happy minutes watching the majesty of nature onscreen. Unless a pigeon comes on. They really just are the worst. 'But Peggy,' you may well say, 'how often do they make a David Attenborough documentary about pigeons?' Two words for you: Rock. Doves. The common ancestor of both domestic and feral pigeons. Pretty much any bird nesting in a cliff is a no-no. And to be honest, I'm not really keen on anything that's even a little bit pigeonish. So that's essentially most birds. If I see a bird during a David Attenborough programme I calmly go and stand next to the television shouting, 'Bird! There's a bird there. A bird! A bird is there! Get the bird!'

When I need to know I can watch something bird-free, I resort to old favourites. Who doesn't love Crufts? Watching a selection of good dogs lead their owners round the ring trying to encourage them to do a little bit of cardio, even though the owners always seem to refuse to try the seesaws or even the cones.

But sometimes we all need something a little more soothing. And since age is just a number, don't rule out the incredible world of children's TV. From *Bluey* to *Paw Patrol*, it's a universal truth that if you want to teach your young how to grow up right, listen to a hound. And while we're on the subject of inspirational viewing, you can't go far wrong with Tom Hardy reading a bedtime story on CBeebies. Now there's someone who has big dog energy.

As I say, try and watch a wide variety of content. Go and see films with superhero dogs in. Pay to download films with superhero dogs in. Multiple times. Buy merchandise with superhero dogs on. And see if you can refresh your social circle. Find new people. Take them to the cinema to see films with dogs in. Only that way will the media moguls realise that people don't need any more cats on screen.

As you can see, curiosity is an infinite gift we can all give to ourselves in every part of our lives.

So, if you are someone who has a saying about not being curious named after you, perhaps, instead of parading back and forth along the fence at the end of the garden like you own the place. Maybe you should take a long hard look at yourself in the mirror? And don't do that thing where you massively inflate yourself up and arch your back, so you look much bigger than you actually are. Be honest. Look at yourself as your actual size. Or better yet, go and get in the sink and make yourself wet so you look like a pathetic soggy radiator. Then look at yourself.

And I would just like you to consider, which one of us is literally referred to as their best friend. And that's not 5,000 years ago by people who wrote it down with little pictures. That's now.

Make sure you stay curious. But in the right way.

Lesson 12: Smell everything

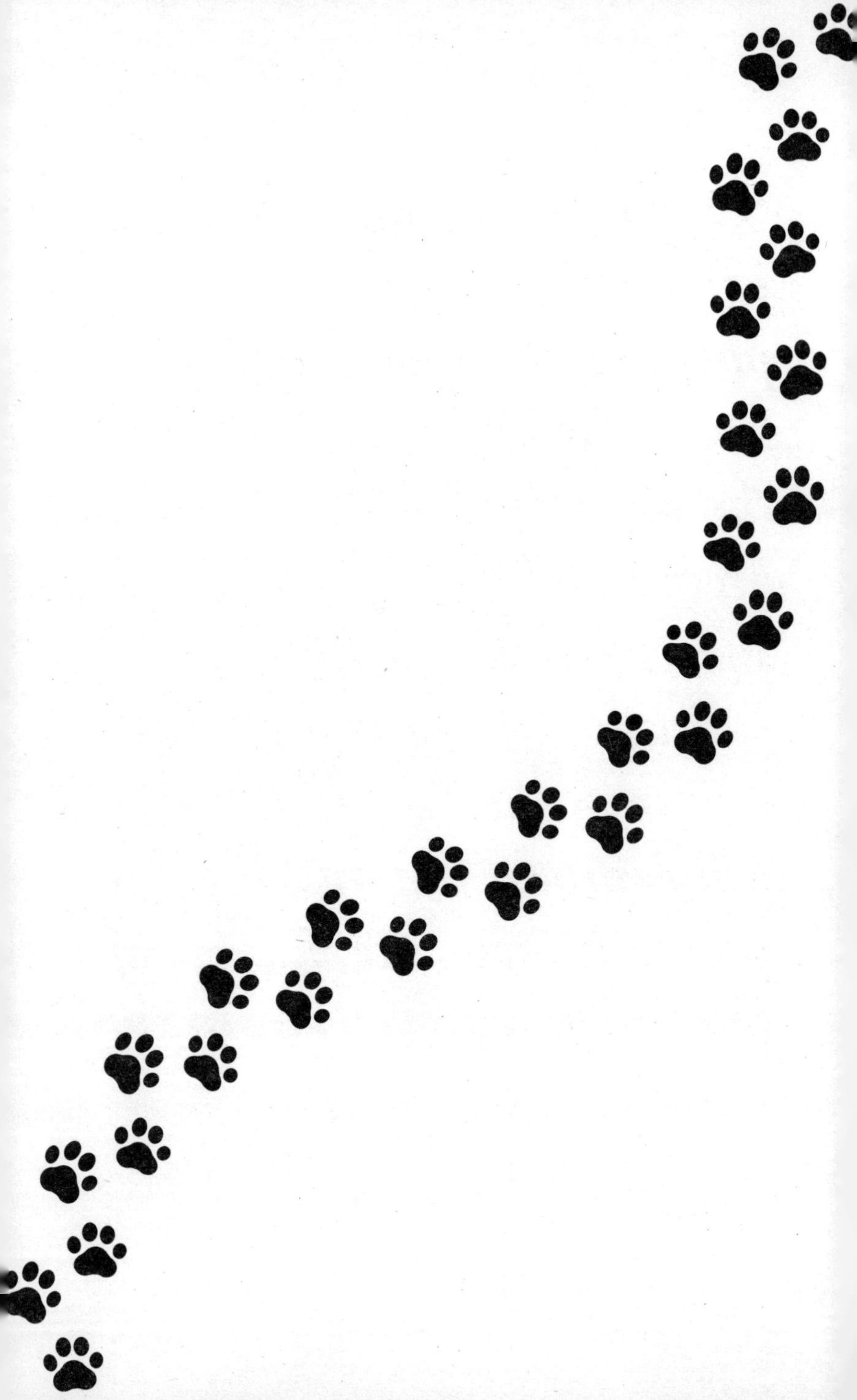

'Open your mind – and your nose – to all possibilities. How do you know the truly good smells: the roast dinner, the sea breeze, the freshly laundered sheets – if you're not benchmarking them against the unwashed sock, the over-full compost bin and my personal favourite, the bit of old kebab on a pavement?'

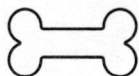

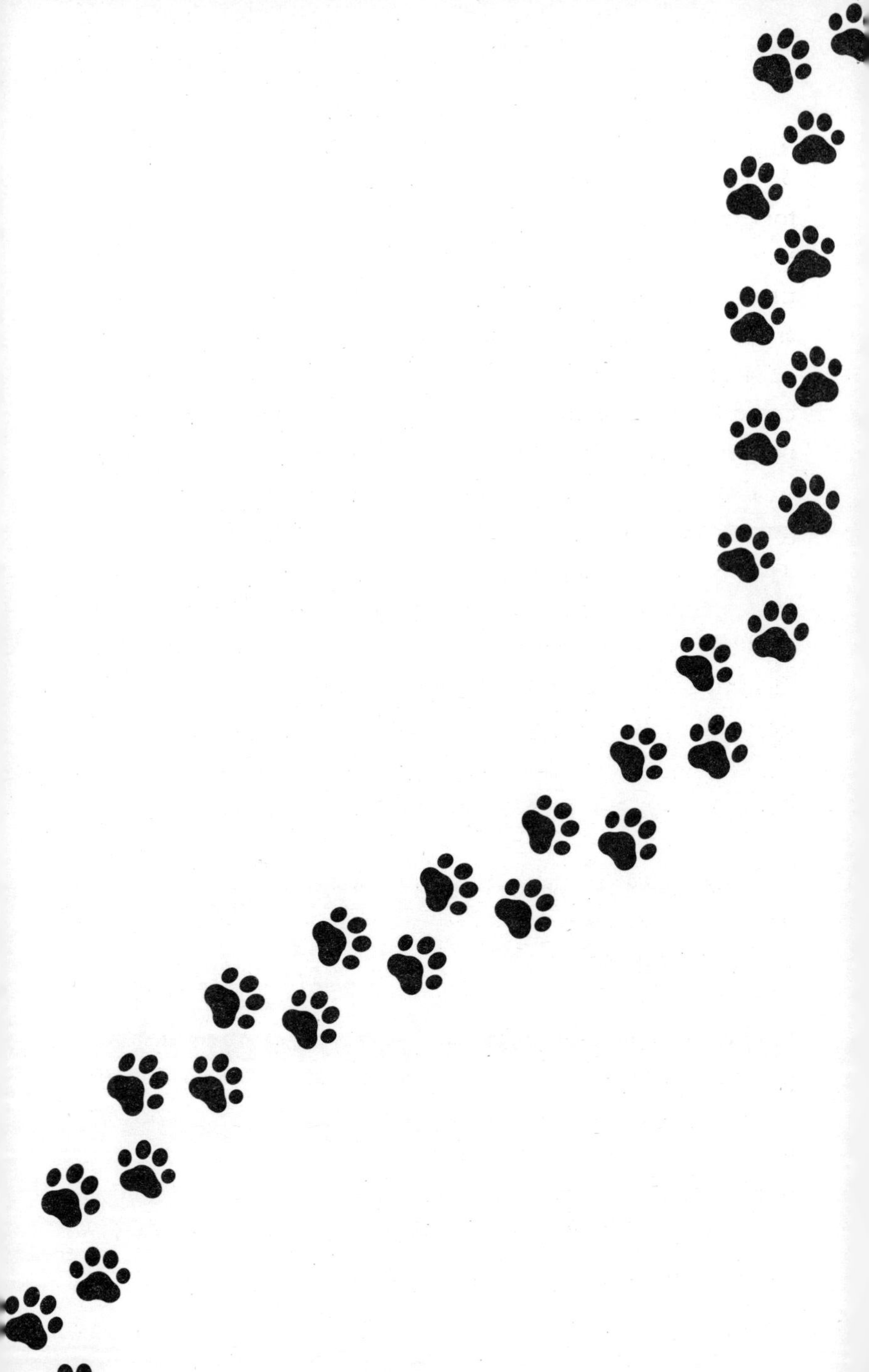

Humans have a rubbish sense of smell. That's not just my opinion. That's science. Whether it's the number of scent receptors, or the size of the olfactory bulb in our brains, our sense of smell is estimated anywhere between 100,000 and 100 million times better than yours. We can smell half a teaspoon of sugar in an Olympic swimming pool. I'm not entirely sure why that would be necessary. I suppose, if someone had a severe sugar allergy it could be quite useful. But they don't normally allow dogs near most swimming pools. And, though I'm all for inclusivity, if you're so allergic to sugar that half a teaspoon in a swimming pool is going to set you off, then you've probably got bigger problems. There's basically more sugar than that everywhere, all the time. Just going to a café must be like playing Russian Roulette for you. And then, let's say it's a swimming pool they let dogs near, we've identified there's sugar in the pool. I'm just not sure what we then do about it. We might have powerful noses but that doesn't actually help us get the sugar back out of the pool does it? Maybe we could boil the water away, retrieve the sugar sediment and then refill the pool with fresh water? But that would take hours, by which point, maybe you're just better off not having a swim today. The point, I suppose, is that dogs would have the option. And life is all about options, isn't it?

Anyway, our lives are suffused with odour. Constantly. You think you know what smells are because you walk past a fishmonger's or have to dodge Dave at work's farts the morning after curry Thursday, but seriously, you have no idea. To be a dog is to be surrounded by smells going off around us like a fireworks display. Fizzing with information. *You* come into a room and might smell that 'something' is baking. *We* come into a room and can smell the butter, the flour, the sugar, the eggs, raw and then cooked, we can smell the person who put the cake in the oven and the stupid little bastard squirrel who walked along the windowsill yesterday like he owned the place. That's why we're constantly sniffing everything, because we're getting a live 3D story about everything that's happened over the last few days. Railings, trees, people, tables, chairs, cars, bins, fences, shoes, hands, jumpers, grass, rocks, trousers, beds, toys. But especially — bumholes.

If you can live your life with a fraction of the curiosity and intensity that we sniff the bumholes of the world, that's a good start, my friend. To be clear, this is (mainly) a metaphor. I'm using this as a way of saying you should seek new experiences constantly. Am I saying that next time you go on a date, you should drop to all fours and go and try and sniff your date *there*? I mean, I'm not, not, not saying you shouldn't. It could be just the sort of bold, decisive, authentic behaviour that they find attractive. After all, you're not going to forget that date in a hurry, are you? And it really would make a great story to tell the grandpuppies.

Here is the other great joy of sniffing. It's the gateway to licking. And then on to chewing. Occasionally I've forgotten the sniffing stage and gone straight to chewing. That one time with the bee was an error. And the pebble that wasn't in fact a mouldy date, but just a pebble. A mistake, I admit. I'm always surprised to see how reluctant humans are to offer a warm lick of greeting. After all, they spend all that time writing greetings card, stuffing them in more paper and licking them — so they seem happy to send their saliva by post, but rarely ever offer it in person. I imagine, not being blessed with the same generosity of tongue as I have been, they're just saving their spittle. I try to do my bit to share the love by offering liberal licks whenever and wherever I can.

Believe me, you should view life as an all-you-can-eat buffet. Sniff every dish. Lick every foot. Chew every sheep poo. Humans spend a lot of time reminding people to 'wake up and smell the coffee' or 'take time to smell the roses' but I think you're missing out on a world of other smells. Open your mind — and your nose — to all possibilities. How do you know the truly good smells: the roast dinner, the sea breeze, the freshly laundered sheets — if you're not benchmarking them against the unwashed sock, the over-full compost bin and my personal favourite, the bit of old kebab on a pavement?

When we choose to focus on the details of now, when we focus on our senses, we begin to practise mindfulness. We improve our mood and how we feel about ourselves in big, important ways. Whether it's gazing for minutes on end at a beautiful leaf, or the pattern on a stone. Or listening to the sound of gentle birdsong. I can vouch for the stillness you get when staring at your human's plate, willing a small morsel to be dropped.

One of the other main ways you can practise mindfulness — and listen, I was as surprised as you to find this out — is to stroke a dog. This isn't just anecdotal, though I'm willing to bet no one ever wished on their deathbed that they'd stroked fewer dogs. This is science. When you stroke a dog, you trigger oxytocin in your brain, a powerful hormone known as the 'cuddle hormone'. It's strongly associated with love bonds, comfort and relaxation. You also produce endorphins, which are strongly linked to a more effective immune system and even increased physical healing.

Now, as my Hollywood stunt coordinator used to say, 'safety is no accident,' so please do your due diligence first. I always recommend approaching a dog's human first to check their employer is open to being stroked. If it were up to me, I'd employ humans to carry around my own personal stroking menu to offer up to my public, as I've always been available for back rubs, belly rubs, pats on the head or even an elegant shake of the paw.

After as little as 10 to 15 minutes of stroking, the levels of the stress hormone cortisol lowers, as do your blood pressure and heart rate. Studies have found that stroking a dog alleviates loneliness and depression, and boosts concentration, focus and encourages a kind of furry mindfulness, as you focus on the task literally at hand (although it's also fine to use your foot in a pinch). Stroking dogs has even been shown to offer benefits to those who have suffered trauma and have serious conditions such as PTSD.

All of the above is true of dogs. I do not know the science as relates to cats but very much doubt there are any benefits at all to touching them.

Lesson 13: Be a big dog

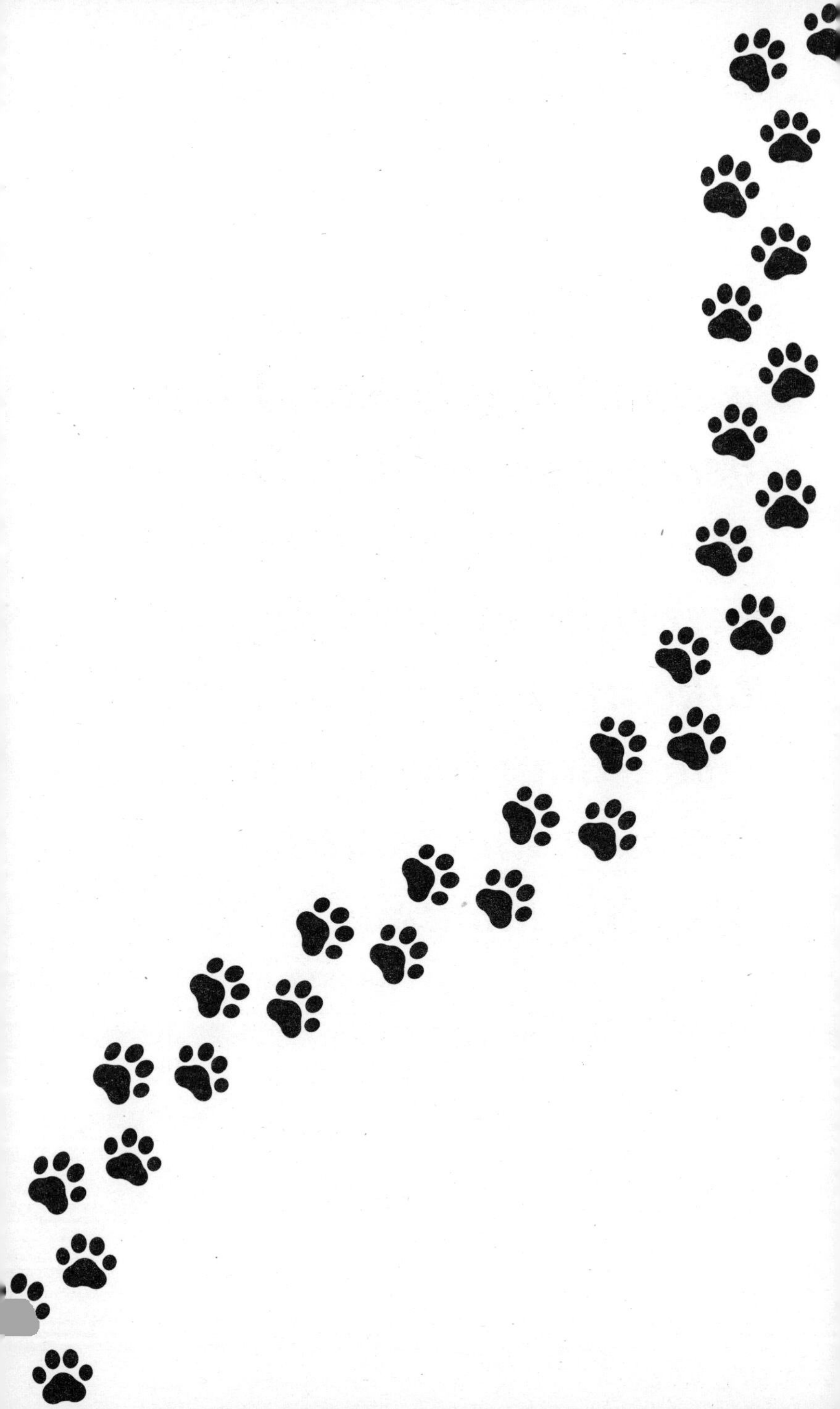

'This is not because being a small dog is bad. I love being a small dog. But we must always operate from a principle of deserving to take up a tiny bit more space than we actually do. Because that is at the heart of being fabulous.'

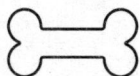

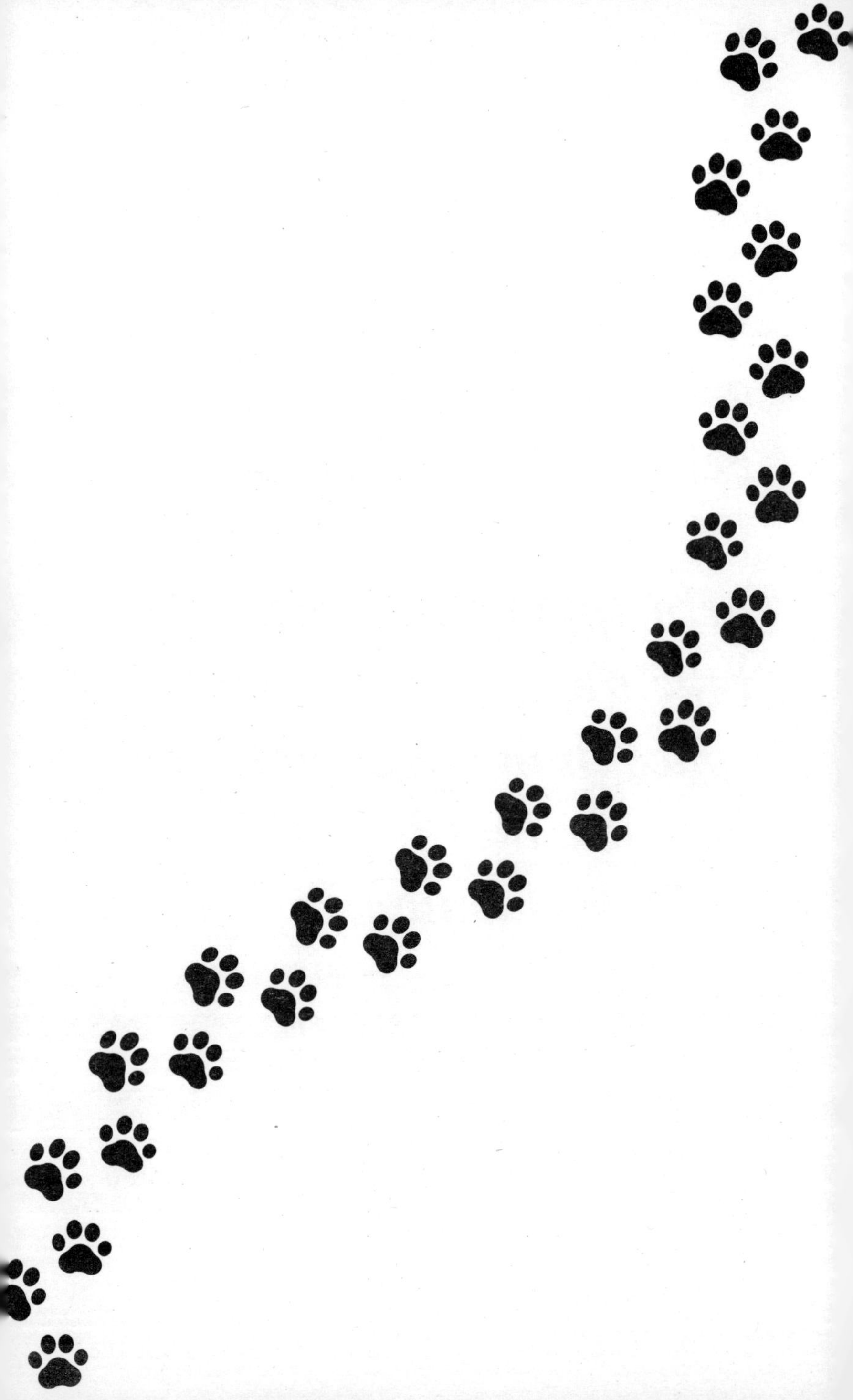

I like to think that part of the reason I'm on speed-dial for so many celebs is down to them being able to rely on my discretion. I pride myself on never engaging in tittle-tattle, I never bark and tell and any green room gossip? I won't whisper a word.

And so it goes that I have a beloved circle of stars to check in on when I'm over in Hollywood. But nonetheless, there are often newcomers and I like to keep up to date.

One fresh-faced star first came to my attention running down Hollywood Boulevard pursued by a pack of yelping Bichon Frises. Even then, his feet slapping against the sidewalk, his elbows frantically pistoning to no great effect, there was something compelling about him. I asked my companion, 'Who is that dear boy?' My chaperone told me the actor in question was still new in town at this point but everyone was already talking about this fierce new talent who looked as if a mop and a lemur had produced an offspring. To me he had the bewitching energy of a handsome cartoon rat in a period film. You could imagine him with his little rat sword and his rat pantaloons, having adventures. What I'm saying is, he had real ghost of a small Dickensian boy, trapped in the body of a low-level crystal meth dealer in contemporary Florida energy. You know, the flirtiest TB patient on the ward. Or perhaps the musketeer we no longer talk about. What I'm trying to say is that his face is a beautiful Italian leather bicycle saddle, surrounded by hair only a toddler with a too large collection of brown crayons could conceive of.

We hurried after him and after I had a few stern words with his doggy pursuers, he stood panting in front of me. It transpired that this particular gang had been menacing him regularly for weeks and he had taken to saving the bacon rind from his brunches to try and negotiate safe passage. But of course, you must never negotiate with terrorists (interestingly though, had it been terriers who had been chasing him, it would have been fine as they're extremely transactional).

That morning, I told it to him straight. 'A tip, you must act like a big dog, even if you're a little dog.' I told him that being a big dog is a state of mind. And I would urge you too to always remember that. Instead of *fake it till you make it*, you need to *bark it till you walk it*. (You have to pronounce walk in a bit of a weird way to make it rhyme with bark, but I maintain it still works. And, full disclosure, am in the process of trademarking it.)

When we act like we're a big dog, the universe believes us. It sends us big dog energy. It gives us big dog things. Our bodies release hormones and we feel more confident. It is an open secret in Hollywood. Walk into any waiting room for an audition in town and you'll find any number of actors striding about and striking power poses. I would, however, recommend rather than manspreading and standing like you've left the coat hangers in your clothes, you could just recite to yourself: I am a big dog. Think of the hackles, the power of four paws, a tail so magnificent it's worth chasing. You will soon feel the Big Dog Energy suffusing you.

I did once also suggest that humans might feel better if they too sported shiny wet noses, but no one has yet been brave enough to try, as far as I know.

From time to time, though, it can lead to unfortunate mishaps. I remember hearing that they got into dreadful difficulties on the set of *Marley & Me* because human actors became so obsessed with achieving pack dominance over the twenty-two different Labrador Retrievers who played Marley. Or when some world leaders insisted on addressing Michael D Higgins, the President of Ireland, first, before even acknowledging his faithful mountain hounds who accompany him everywhere. A tip for everyone — channel the Big Dog, but accept you will never be more Big Dog than an actual Big Dog.

Remember, none of this is because being a small dog is bad. I love being a small dog. But we must always operate from a principle of deserving to take up a tiny bit more space than we actually do. Because that is at the heart of being fabulous. One of the great curses in life is imposter syndrome. The feeling that we do not deserve to be where we are. That at any moment, everyone is going to realise you don't belong in your own success. But trust me. You do. That feeling that you are an imposter, that is the robust level of self-doubt that any sensitive, thoughtful person has. Rather than disqualifying you from success, my dear, it is the reason why you will achieve it. I don't want to pretend it's easy. But I promise you, you will get there.

When I won my Fido award (people tend to call these the Oscars of the dog acting world, but I like to think the Oscars are the pale imitation of the Fidos), up against so many other canine actors, I admit I had a moment where I wondered if I truly deserved the award (and then, if truth be told, I had another moment of outrage when I realised I'd been nominated in the comedy category rather than 'Best Onscreen Kiss,' which was where I felt my performance really excelled. The tongue. It's all about the tongue, I tell you). But then when I not only received that award but the overall prize, I knew I had to take my imposter syndrome by the scruff of the neck and throw it out. I deserved to step into my Big Dog Power.

So ever since then, I love to help fledgling stars find that energy for themselves. That day, when I spotted that fresh-faced star being chased by the Bichon Frise, looking around furtively in case the pack returned, there and then we made a deal. We would organise a monthly brunch and I would help him unleash his inner big dog. Painstakingly, brunch by brunch, sausage by sausage, I was able to coax his inner big dog into life. It took all sorts of techniques, from withholding his bacon, to shaking a water bottle full of gravel in his face, which he hated. But we got there. Within six months, there wasn't a Bichon Frise in the whole of Hollywood who was going to mess with him.

Now, before that actor does anything else, he stands and stares at himself in the mirror saying 'Big Dog Energy! Big Dog Energy! Big Dog Energy!' The volume increasing as his eyes become wilder and wilder, his mane of unkempt hair shaking and quivering like a wild dog. Then he does a long, piercing wolf howl.

And before you dismiss this as Hollywood tomfoolery, you try it. No one who's ever had a good howl at the sky has ever regretted it.

Lesson 14: You be you

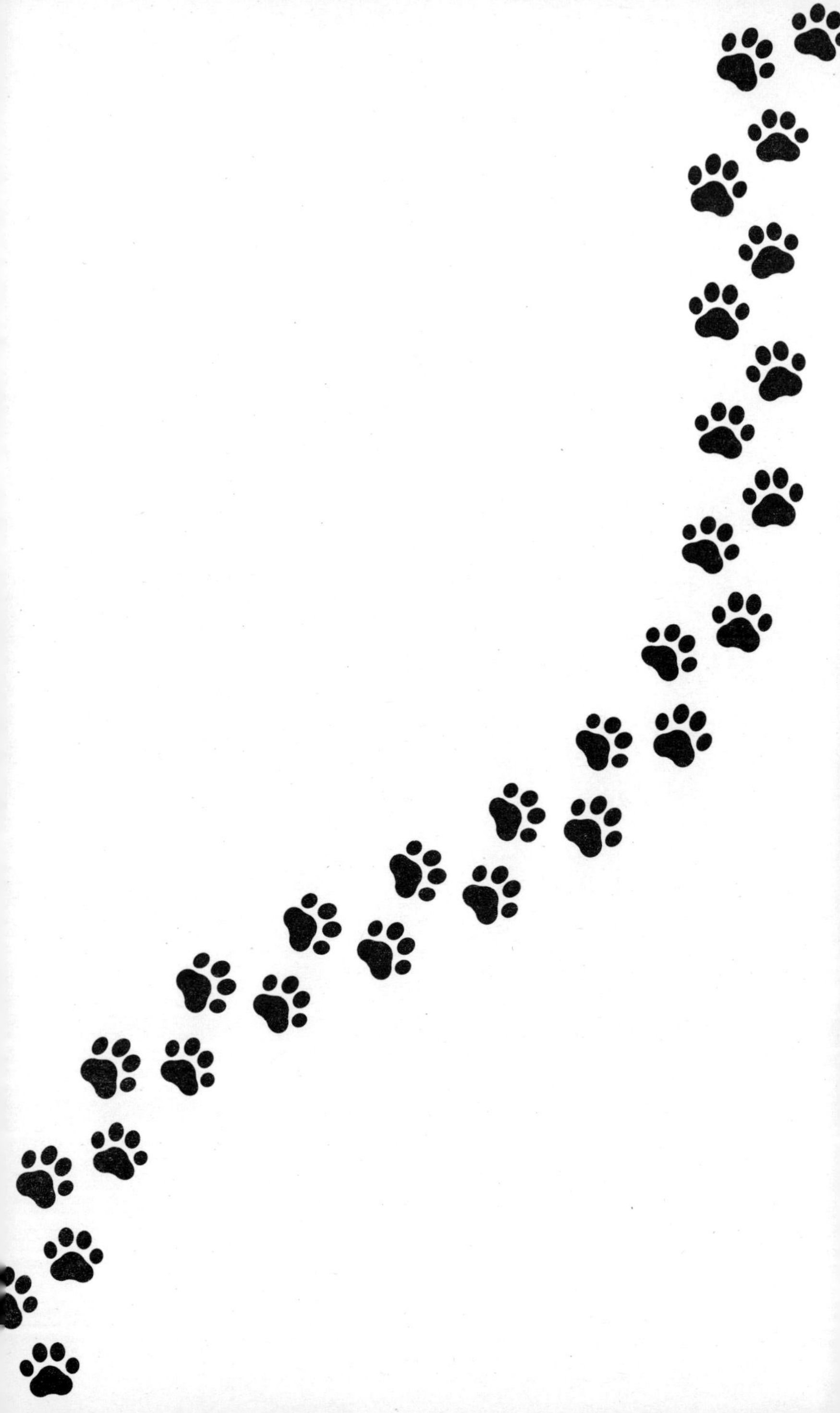

'The fact that you exist now, as you, reading this sentence, is a miracle. Even if you do only have two nipples. So you'd better start acting like you're a miracle. Anything else would be a waste of all of our time.'

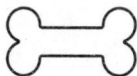

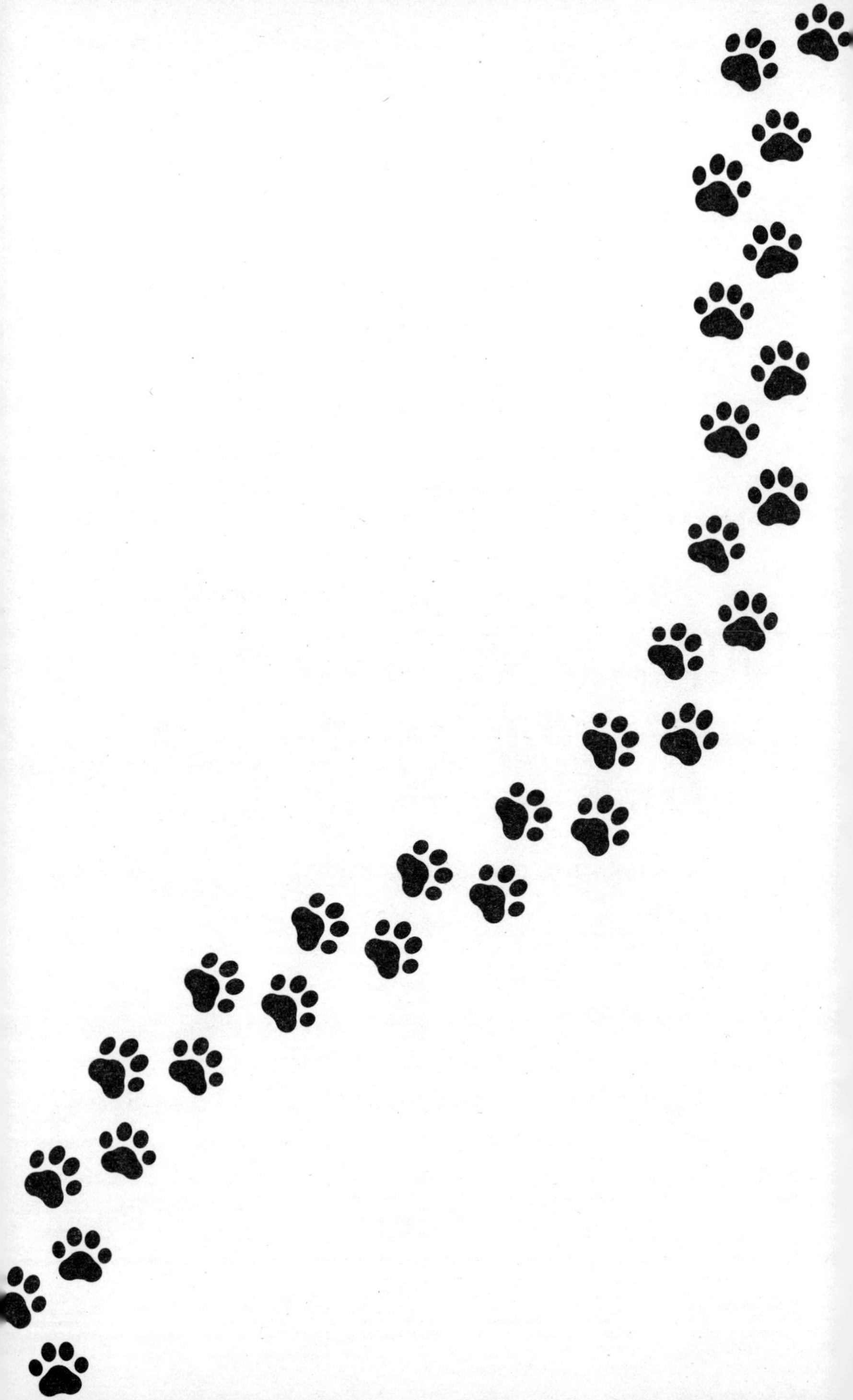

Y ou may have heard the saying 'Be the person your dog thinks you are'. I get it. You think, because of how we treat you, how excited we are to see you, that we must think you're this amazing person, someone better and more deserving than you actually believe yourself to be. This phrase is essentially a short-hand for you trying to be the best version of yourself. And, listen, I'm a big fan of positive thinking and affirmation. It's another key to being fabulous. A key part of my *bark it till you walk it* (remember you have to do a kind of New York taxi driver accent to make the two words rhyme satisfyingly) philosophy, is the idea that we must actively treat ourselves well. It's not enough to just think it. We must tell ourselves. And then act on it.

So believe the hype: we have the strength to overcome any challenge. We have the talent to make the most of all opportunities that come our way. We are all worthy of love and respect. We do deserve a tummy rub. When we consistently voice these sorts of positive messages, we increase our ability to be kind and compassionate to ourselves and also to other people. The point is not to make the grandest biggest statement that you can think of, but instead to make these goals achievable. We all have that little voice in our head telling us that we are not enough. Or that we are too much. That we don't look the way we should or sound the way we want to.

Perhaps you have a tiny tongue, or too much fur? Or oddly tiny nipples? Well that is what makes you you. But that's not a problem. That's not something to apologise for. That's a cause for wonder. The chances of the exact occurrence of factors as every one of your ancestors met and had children to produce you, now in this moment has been estimated at one in 400 trillion. They had to survive wars and plagues and natural disasters along the way. The fact that you exist now, as you, reading this sentence, is a miracle. Even if you do only have two nipples. So you'd better start acting like you're a miracle. Anything else would be a waste of all of our time.

But that doesn't mean that we should stop trying to grow and develop and be the best version of ourselves. I'm always striving for the next challenge — the world nap record, perhaps, or persuading all the world's pigeons they should start a colony on the moon. Find your strengths and play to them.

Once you've acknowledged your strengths, use them. Find your vocation. When you're working for a cause you believe in, you'll find the motivation comes naturally. I've been lucky enough to travel the world, but wherever I go, I always try to visit a local rescue dog home and the incredible people that run them. I can't imagine my life without Luke and Holly, and it breaks my doggy heart to think of pups and good boys and dignified (and not so dignified) ancient doggos without a forever home, so I always try to raise funds to ensure no dog goes short of a biscuit on my watch.

Through my work as Dogpool, I've also had the good fortune to join the wild and wonderful world of conventions. These astonishing communities of fans and actors are a joy to behold. While I admit I was, at first, a little surprised by the under-representation of the canine community at these events, I've come to cherish my status as a wildcard there. I love to sign a pawtograph while meeting fans. But the surprise part I've come to love is the incredible passion poured into the costumes. Whose heart wouldn't lift to see a life-size Groot taking a Diet Coke break or Darth Vader stopping to tie his shoelace. But one thing I've learned is that these amazing fans often aren't dressing up to be someone else — but to channel a part of themselves they've always wanted to share.

Sometimes an outfit isn't a disguise or a mask (apart from when it is an actual mask, I suppose) — sometimes clothes and costumes are at the heart of self-expression. You could dress like everyone else. But where's the fun in that? Your fashion is an extension of you. It's playful, expressive, inclusive. It can be as simple as the right colour or as complicated as a bespoke dress. It all depends on mood.

My wardrobe is an explosion of colour and texture. Some days I'm all about being cozy with homely knits — very hygge, very grounded. The next I might feel more Harry Styles energy: feather boas, sequins, and unapologetically bold choices. A little bit of Harris Tweed when on a hike in Scotland, a bit of bling and sportswear when I'm feeling more street. I like to rise to the occasion — a full ballgown for a premiere, or a bold Christmas jumper in the festive season. But sometimes, even a style icon like me will admit that on occasion, less is more. I've always been blessed with body confidence — which is a good thing, with no cloak of fur to hide in — but I know not everyone would feel as carefree as I do, strolling down the street naked apart from a jaunty hat, or pair of sunglasses, and I realise humans are generally discouraged from walking around in their birthday suit, but in the privacy of your own home, why not try the Peggy way some-times? Not a stitch apart from a jazzy bandana. It's a summer mood.

I like to take inspiration from everything around me when it comes to style. But whether it's head-to-toe designer or a battered old hoodie, remember that you're wearing it and that's what matters.

Because I want to let you in on a secret. We've been there when you're singing along to a song on the radio. We've watched you dance around the kitchen. We've listened to you have imaginary conversations with your socks. We've witnessed you practising facial expressions in the mirror. We've watched you build forts out of sofa cushions and shout at the TV. We've heard you laughing till you can't breathe because you did such a loud fart. (I am a very great believer that you should always fart, whenever you have the opportunity.)

We've sat with you on the sofa when you've been in yesterday's clothes eating a party pack of cocktail sausages straight from the packet. (Yes, that's partly because we're hoping you'll drop one.) But it's also because we want to be there for you. Not just for the sunny days in the park. But for all the rainy days, too. We know your flaws and your tangles and your difficulties. We still turn our head to the side when you talk to us. We still feel so safe that we sleep with our legs pointed up into the air. And we still rest our heavy heads on you. We lean against you. We follow you from room to room, looking up at you. We lick you with love. Again, and again. Not because we have this perfect version of you in our heads. But because we see you. As you are. And that is everything we need.

So be the person you are. We'll still love you.

Lesson 15: Why settle for 'good'?

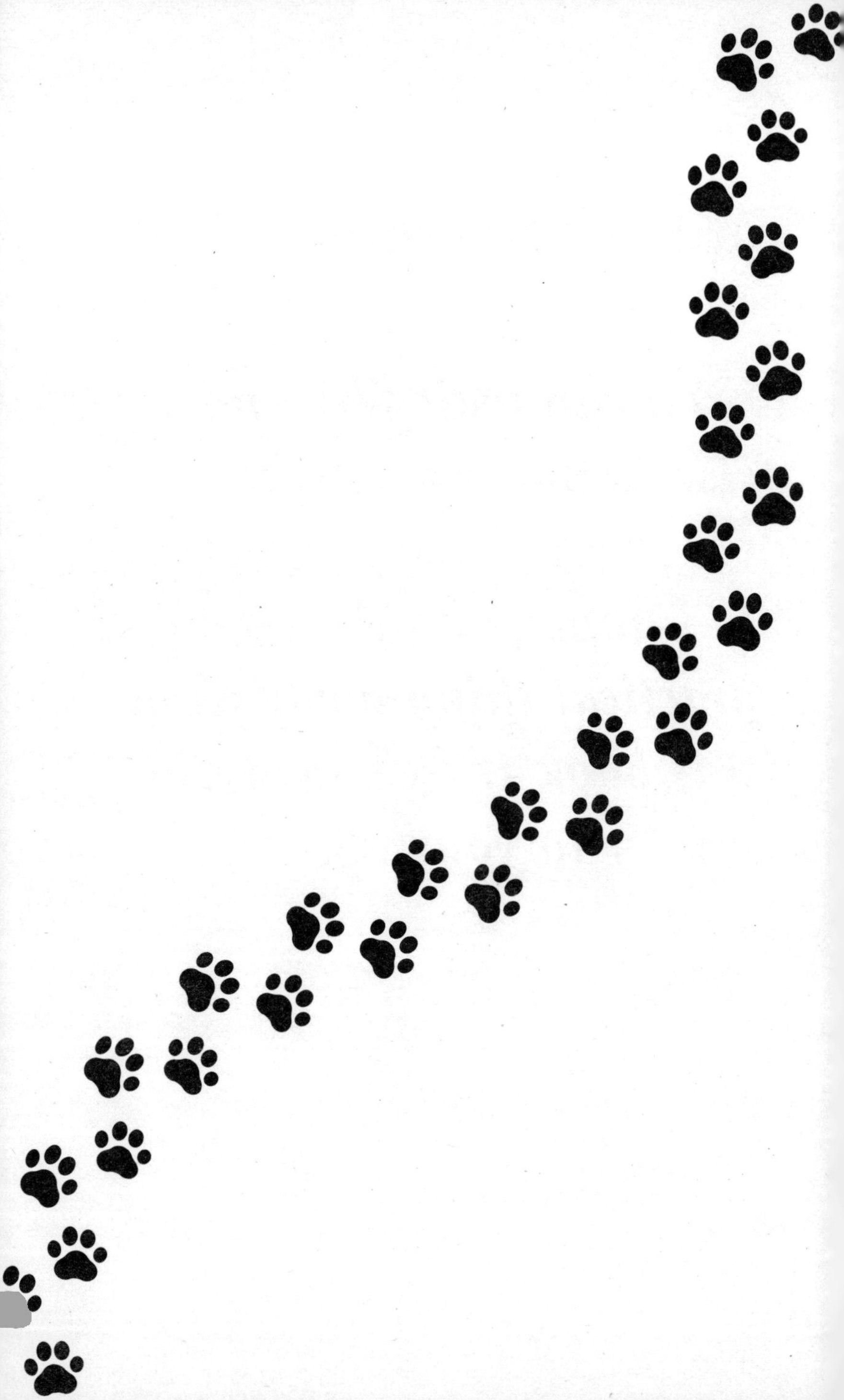

'You can wait for someone else to pat you on the head. Or you can do it yourself. If I hope you take one practical thing away from this book it is for you to be kinder to yourself.'

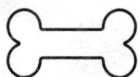

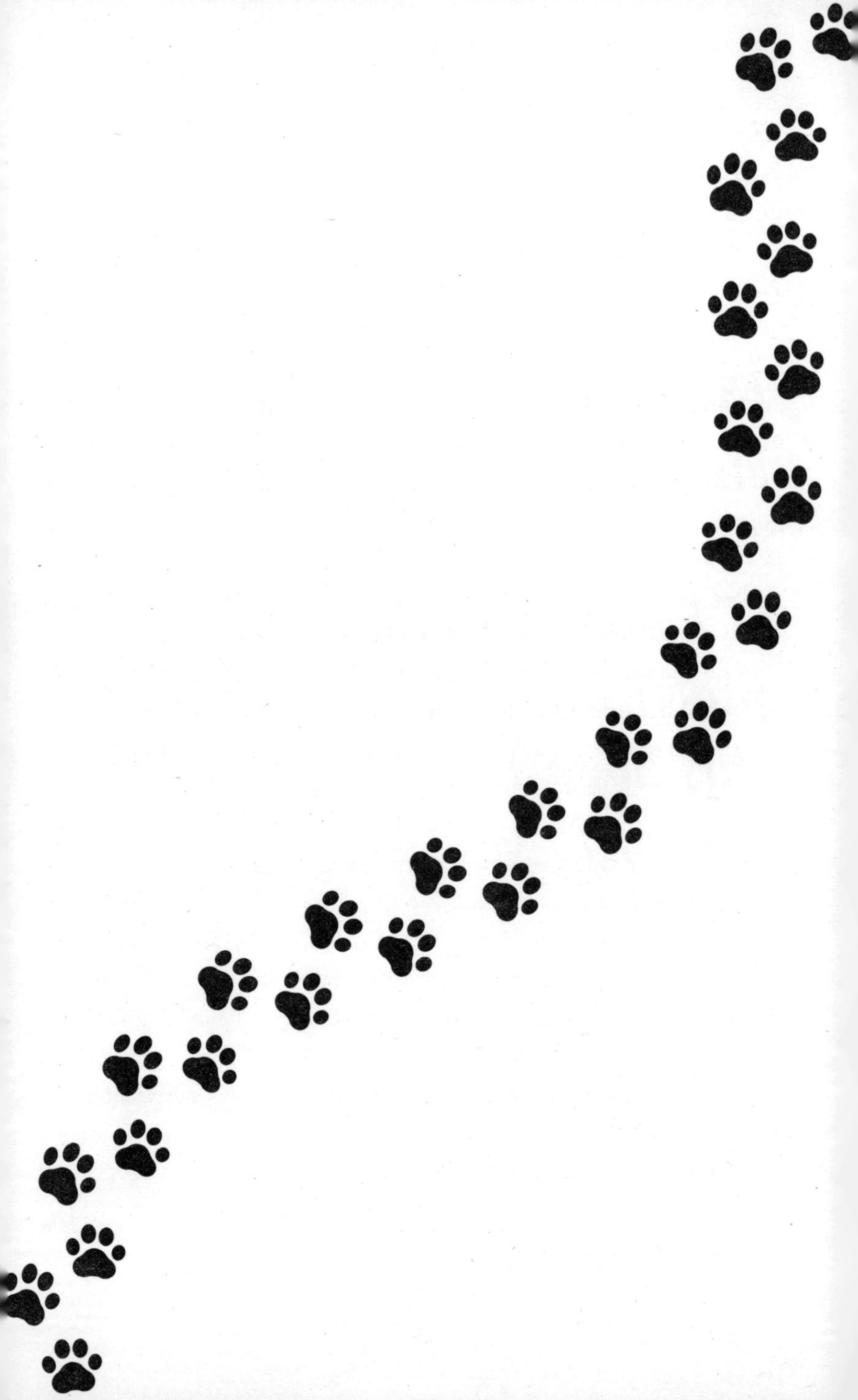

Good and dog. Two words that go together. Two words that make the world go round. They just feel right together. Like vanish and squirrel. Good. Dog.

And for most of my young life, I chased being a good dog and avoided being a called a bad dog. Although, I realised there are occasions when being not so much a bad dog, but a mad dog, are called for. You might think that only biker chiefs and wrestlers take on the Mad Dog moniker, but I say we all need to find our inner mad dog occasionally. I'm not one to growl as a rule, but occasionally, if I spot a dog's human NOT doing their duty on the poo-picking front, or even contemplating leaving their dog in a car on a warm day ... then this mad dog is howling.

But generally, I'm a peace-loving Peg. It's cool to be cool, and in my youth, all I wanted was to be the Good Dog. That was enough for me. Whether I was sitting, laying, fetching, staying, or heeling, it became my lodestar, the way that I navigated everything. But then, a few years back, I was at a lunch with Hollywood royalty. I forget what it was for, but there was a big gaggle of producers and actors and agents. Anyway, this legendary actor was just about to leave and as he was given his keys by the valet they said, 'You have a good day, sir,' and he replied, 'No, you have an *excellent* day.' And with that he was gone, in a roar of motorcycle fumes and the pungent whiff of wisdom. I caught the eye of the carparking guy and we both just had our mouths open. Had we heard right? We both mouthed it to ourselves. 'Have an *excellent* day.'

That night, as I lay listening to recordings of Taylor Swift telling me about her love life, I kept turning it over and over in my mind. I felt like those first humans who heard Copernicus proposing the heliocentric universe. As if someone had taken existence apart and put it back together in a slightly different order.

The next morning, I was at a brunch and the server asked me how my food was. 'Superb, Katalina,' I said. 'Superb.' From that day onwards, I made a promise to myself that good was no longer enough. The world is a much richer place when we embrace the nuance of all of our excellence. But this should not be a silent process. We need to tell it to ourselves out loud, every day. When we speak a positive truth about our lives and experiences out loud, we activate parts of our brain connected to our reward system. We lower our threat response and we literally rewire our brain to think more kindly about ourselves.

Try it out for size. Next time you pass an Afghan hound, with hair swishier than Gwyneth Paltrow, tell them how glorious they look. Spotted an Old English Sheepdog the size of a small sofa? Tell them they're marvellous. Compliment a Poodle on its pomp, a Labrador on its lapping, a Bulldog on its bounciness. See the nice thing, say the nice thing and it's nailed-on neuroscience that you'll notice more nice things.

And don't leave yourself out. You can wait for someone else to pat you on the head. Or you can do it yourself. If I hope you take one practical thing away from this book it is for you to be kinder to yourself. To take the opportunity every time you pass a mirror to say something nice to yourself. Don't focus on how dry your nose is, instead notice the colour of your eyes. Don't be so tough on yourself for not having enough wrinkles. Remember — it's not that you are insufficiently wrinkly, full-stop, it's more that you're working on it. And one day, you too will have a marvellous array of crumples and rumples like me.

Lesson 16: Share your couch

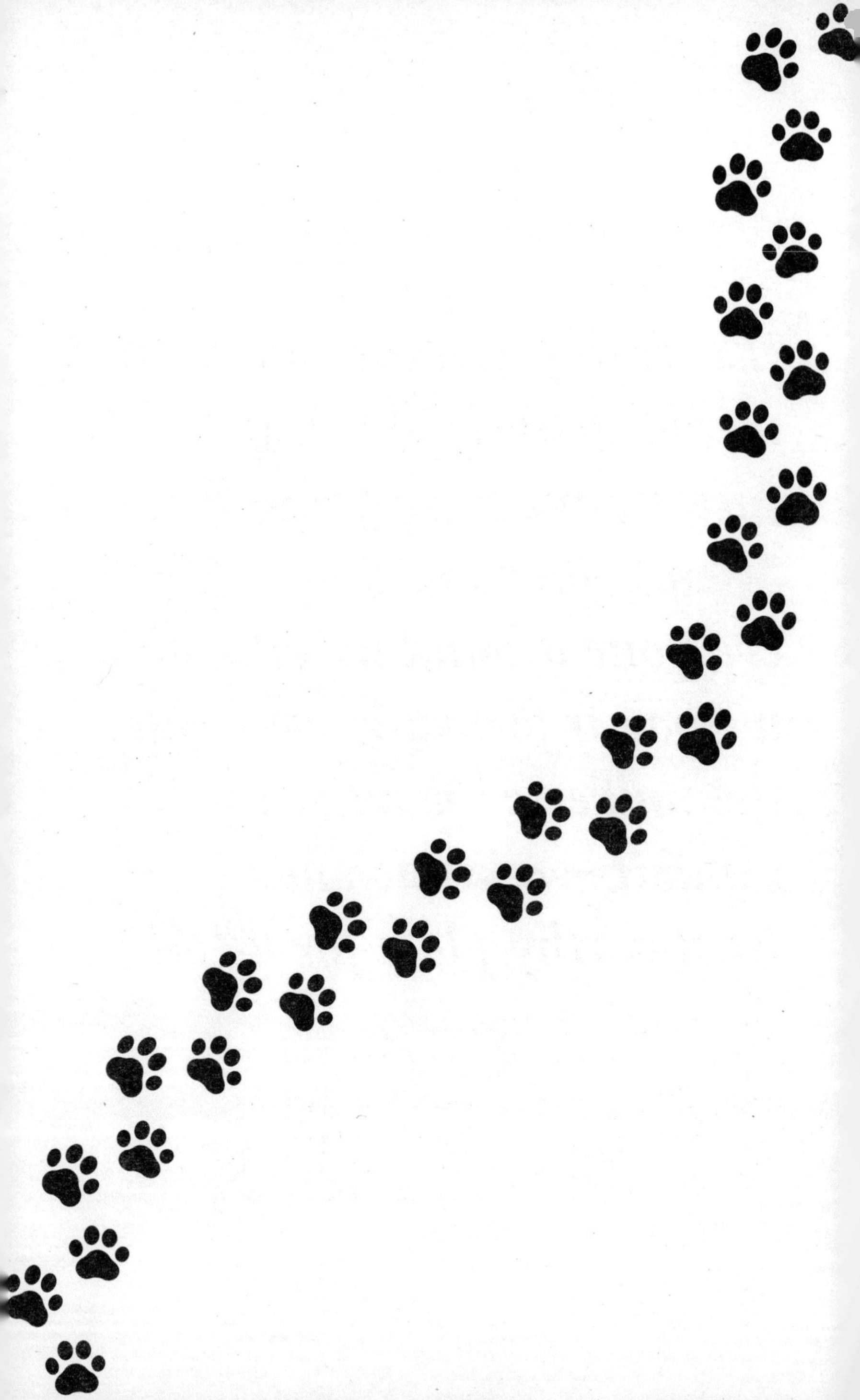

'Learning to share our couch means actively sharing our success, our support and in essence, our love with everyone around us. When we pay it forwards we create the universe we want to inhabit – a kinder, more trustworthy place for us all.'

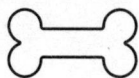

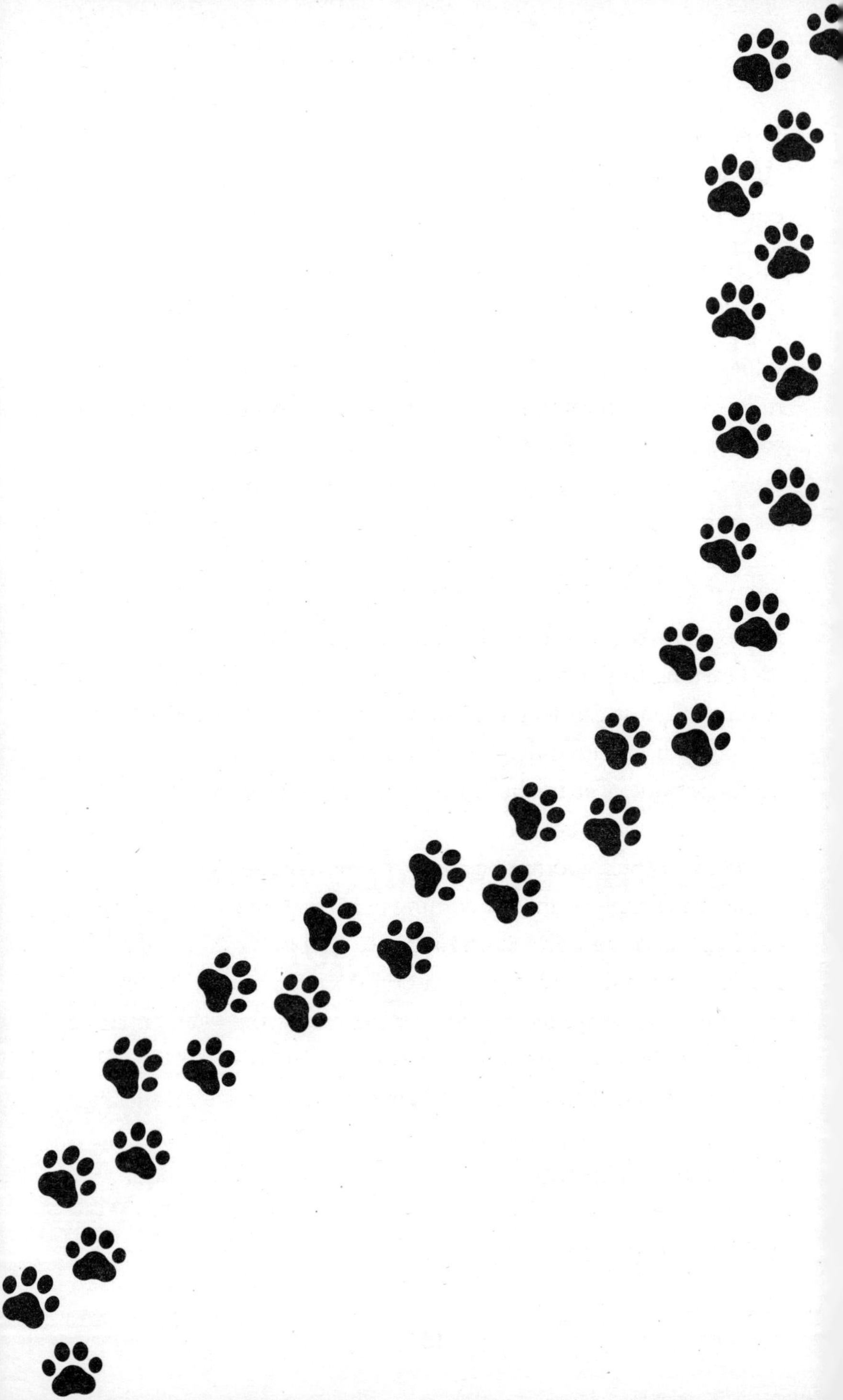

While Holly and Luke have a perfectly respectable couch, which I'm happy to allow them to sit on with me, I confess America has really taken the sofa to a new level. A great Hollywood friend of mine, a film star and former bodybuilder of great stature, has a purpose-built, reinforced sofa, which he had shipped in from the former Soviet Union. It's the most divine, white leather behemoth which stretches on for what feels like miles. It can comfortably seat up to thirty or so people and has a variety of holders for drinks, snacks and countless accessories. It reclines, massages, charges assorted devices and pretty much does everything apart from throw a stick. It's a couch you could live on. But my LA amigo taught me a valuable lesson.

'Always share the couch, Peg,' he once said to me. 'It doesn't matter how big it is. That's the American Dream.'

Learning to share can often be one of the hardest things in life. All too often it can feel as if life is a competition. As if someone else's wealth, success or happiness is somehow taking away from the finite amount of it in the universe. But that is of course untrue. There is an infinite amount of it. There will always be another chew toy, another stick, another bowl of leftover roast chicken. When we growl menacingly at anyone coming near our bowl of leftover roast chicken, we do not project strength, we project weakness and fear. But more than that, when we send this sort of negative energy out into the universe, we receive it in return. Who would you rather be around — the sort of person who welcomes you towards a bowl of leftover roast chicken, or the sort of person who growls in warning? We, all of us, want to surround ourselves with positive, open companions. Negativity sucks the joy and energy out of life.

The game of tug of war is the perfect example here. We think we're in competition, we put our all into trying to be the victor and walking off with the soggy chewed rope. But after we've done it, we realise the joy was in the game, not the triumph. Sharing is caring, my friends. Although I admit I don't know if my humans always feel that when I offer up a delightfully drool-soaked tennis ball to throw. But I will keep on trying.

The truth is that there are countless benefits to this sort of generosity, even if selflessness isn't your thing. It's good for us physically, mentally and emotionally. We get what is known as a helper's high from the blend of serotonin, oxytocin, dopamine and endorphins that doing a good deed gives us. It lowers our stress levels and has been linked to lower levels of anxiety and depression. It enhances our self-esteem, raises our confidence and strengthens our social bonds.

Learning to share our couch means actively sharing our success, our support and in essence, our love with everyone around us. When we pay it forwards we create the universe we want to inhabit — a kinder, more trustworthy place for us all.

I used to think I was not able to share my sofa. I'm a dog that loves to recline, after all. But then I realised the more people that were on my couch, the more pockets there were to sniff for snacks, the greater the chance to get a head scratch and a belly rub simultaneously. I firmly believe that life is a symphony not a solo. It may be a symphony of snores and farts, but the more people on your couch, the richer the harmony.

Lesson 17: Wag this way

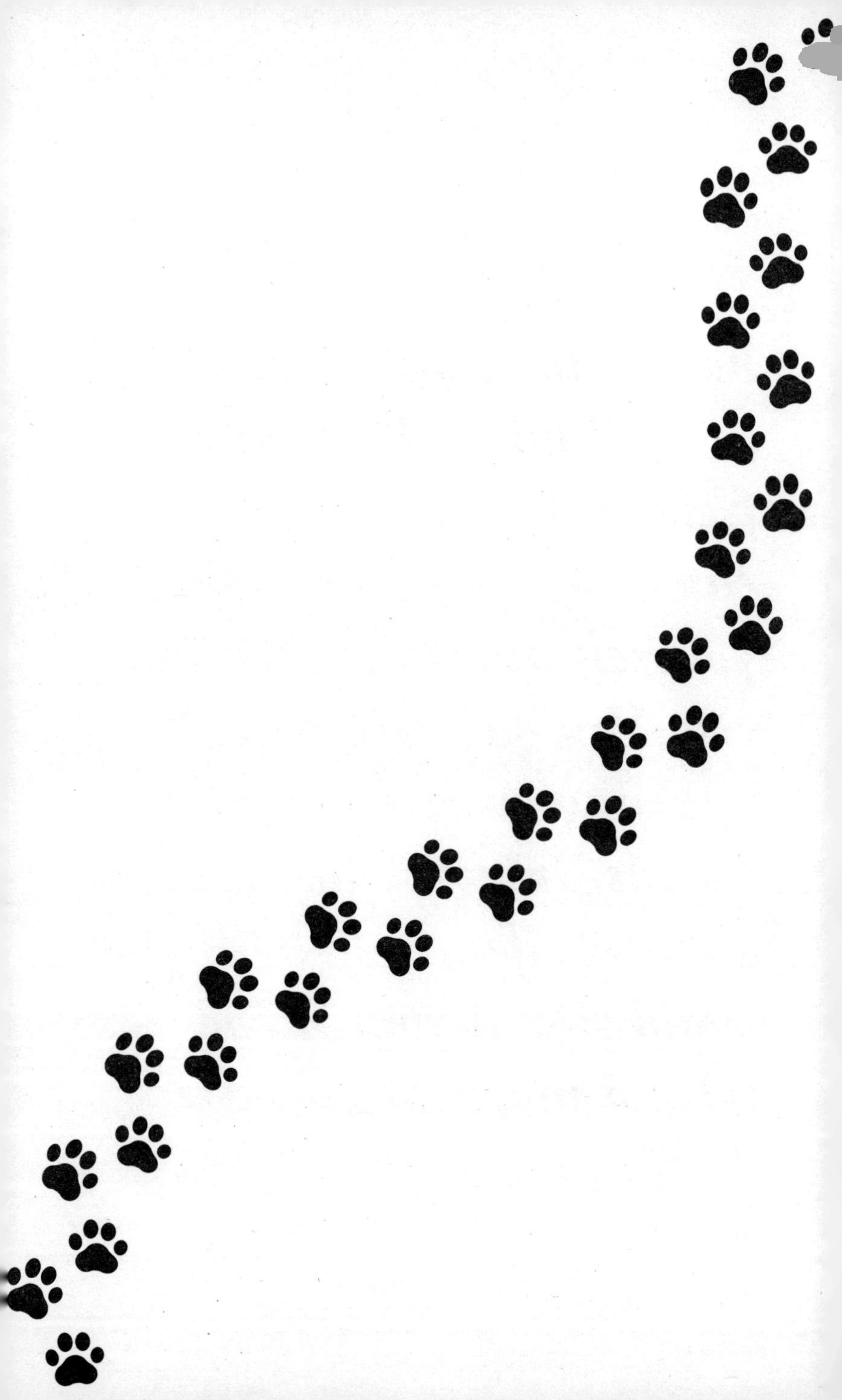

'Humans, you don't even have a tail. You're walking around with all of these feelings and experiences churning around inside yourself and so is everyone else. You go around guessing everyone else's moods. Imagine how much simpler life would be if you could signal your mood with a magnificent tail.'

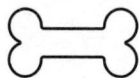

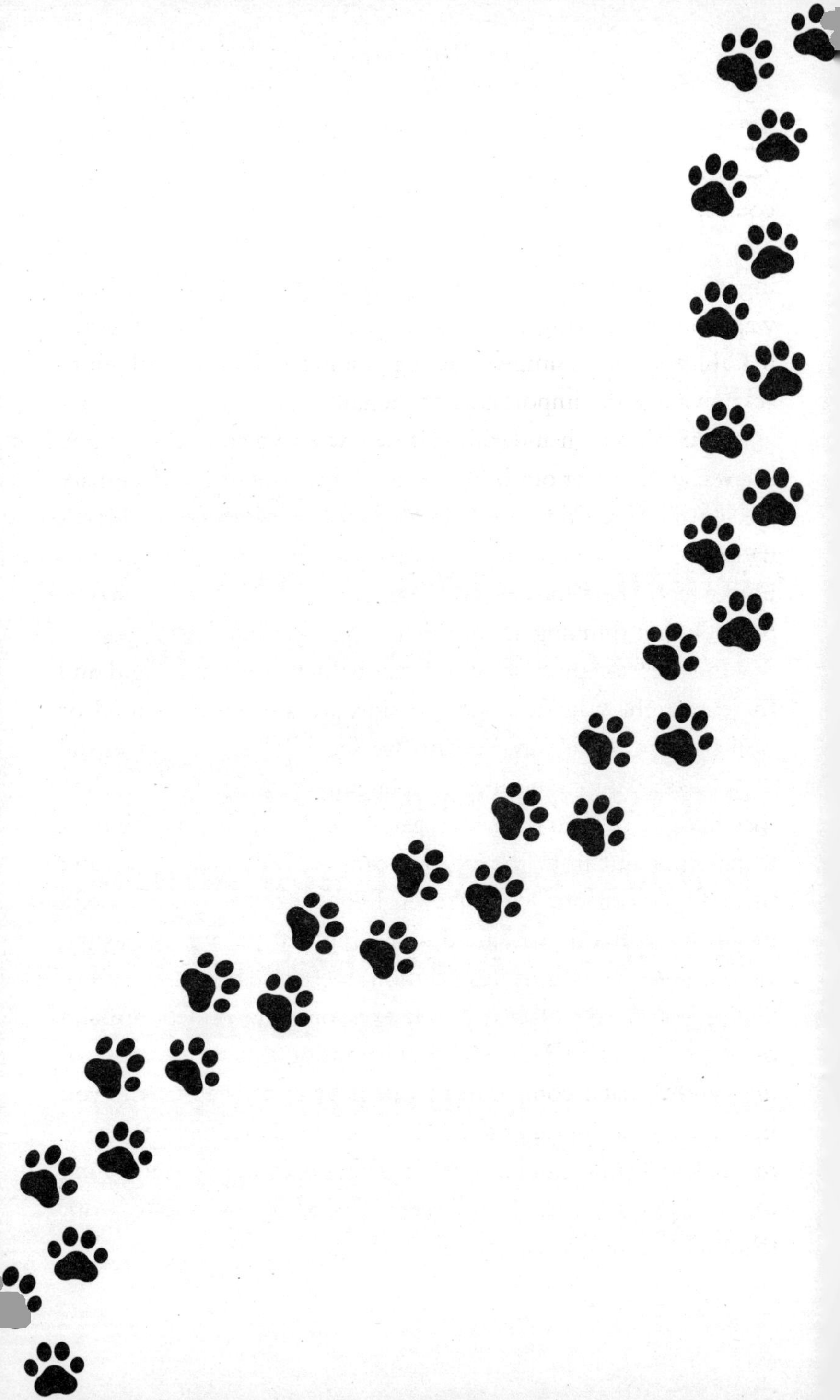

Everyone thinks it's easy to tell if we dogs are happy. Just check the tail. If it's wagging, happy. If it's not, we're not. But, of course, we're far more complicated than that. As an astute human knows, we've got many other ways of sharing our joy — including (but not limited to) licking, singing, jumping, full-body waggling and pawing. And I don't think anyone would disagree that the zoomies is simply pure happiness. But I'd be a fool not to acknowledge the importance of the tail.

If our tail is high and still, or slowly wagging and held upright, or even arched over our back, we are alert, ready to act, or perhaps are signalling our desire for dominance. Of course, some breeds naturally have a high tail, so don't assume a Pomeranian or a Husky feels a certain way. To be honest, with both of them they're probably not thinking about much, if you get my drift.

However, for most of us, if a tail is high, erect and rigid and there's a tight wag from side to side, we are tense, focused or suspicious in some way. Perhaps we see a big ginger cat in the distance, walking along like they literally own the world, when they need to stick to their own garden and wind their neck in. A tail straight out from the body means we're curious. Low and tucked between our legs, or even fully tucked under the belly, means we're anxious or afraid, signalling that we are submissive. Even a tentative wag in this position doesn't change this. And of course, you need to factor in our eyes, our ears, our mouth and our overall posture. But which tail position signals the sense of melancholy that accompanies the memory of a past love, who you never got to say a proper goodbye to? How do we tell you we're more than a little troubled about global warming or mourning the last episode of *Gavin and Stacey*? Good luck trying to work that one out from what our tail is doing.

And with humans, you don't even have a tail. You're walking around with all of these feelings and experiences churning around inside yourself and so is everyone else. You go around guessing everyone else's moods. Imagine how much simpler life would be if you could signal your mood with a magnificent tail. But without such a blessing, no wonder you make such a pig's ear of reading other people's emotions. (No offence to pig's ears. A tasty treat.)

There have been famous studies that repeatedly show that you humans put your *own* actions down to the context but *other people's* actions you attribute to their personality or character. Sorry if I've gone full-on psychologist there but if you snap at someone, you recognise it's because you're tired, you've had a long day, or you have money worries. But if you see someone else snap at someone, it's because they're mean. They're the sort of person who snaps. They're impatient. If you can learn to stop comparing your internal life to the little you can see of other's external lives, we'd all be a lot more tolerant. I mean, it would be easier if you hadn't all just evolved your tails away, but it's too late for that now.

I have learned to never judge someone else. We never know what someone else is going through. You try it. The next time someone bashes the supermarket trolley into your ankles, or cuts in front of you in traffic, imagine all of the hundreds of things that could be going on in their life that might explain their behaviour. Take a deep breath in and out. Then check to see if you still feel as annoyed by it. I bet you don't.

Always remember, you don't have a tail. So you need to use your words. You have to tell people how you are feeling, what you need more of, what you could do with less of. I'm not saying people will always agree with you ('No we can't go for a fourth walk today, Peggy'), but they might at least understand you.

Lesson 18: How to bark up the right tree

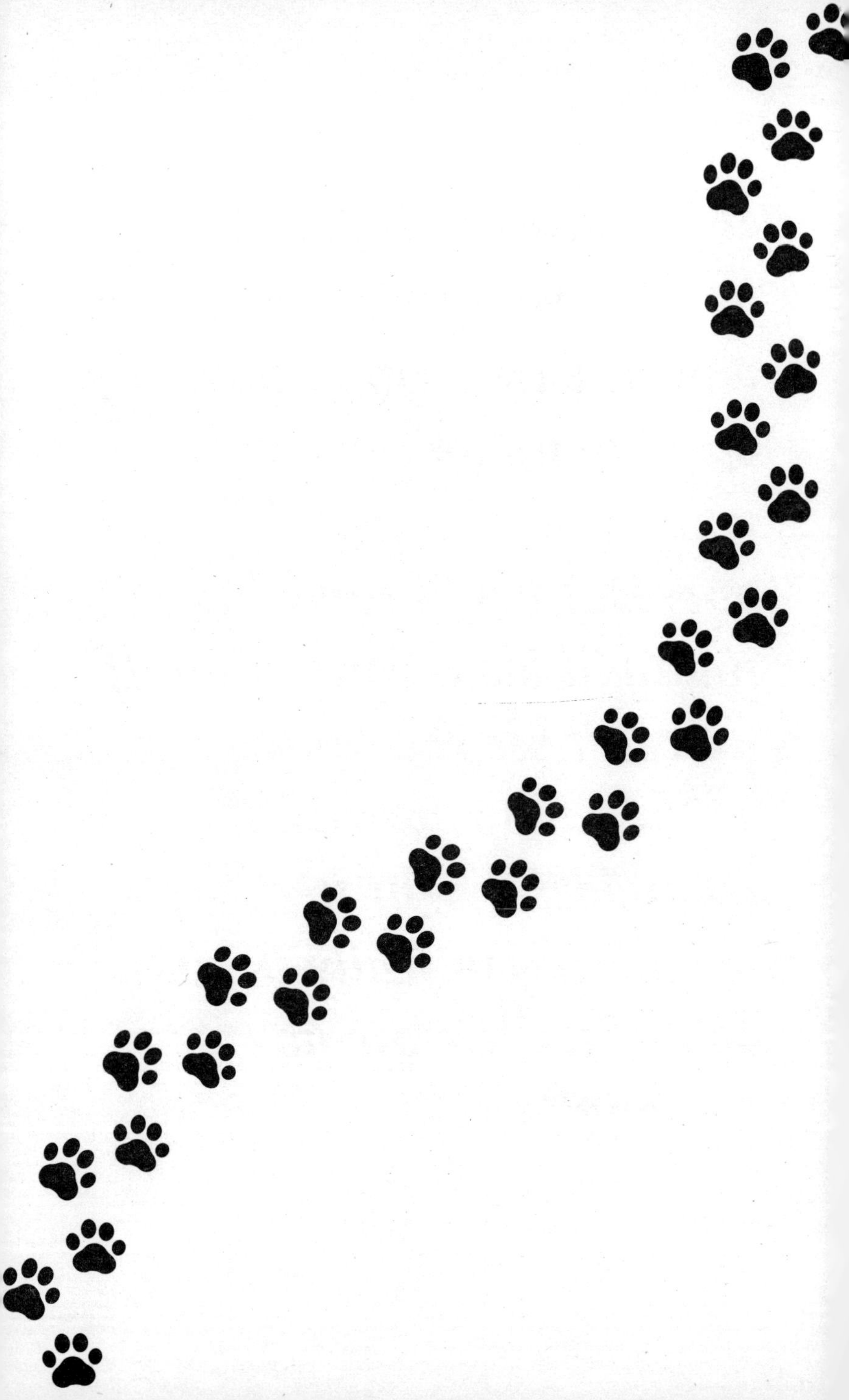

'Life is about finding the balance between staying with the tree you're currently barking up and knowing when to bark up a different one. But here's something that will blow your mind. If we can't see the squirrel up in the canopy anyway then what does "right tree" even mean? If you really think about it, there are no "wrong" trees.'

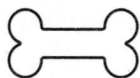

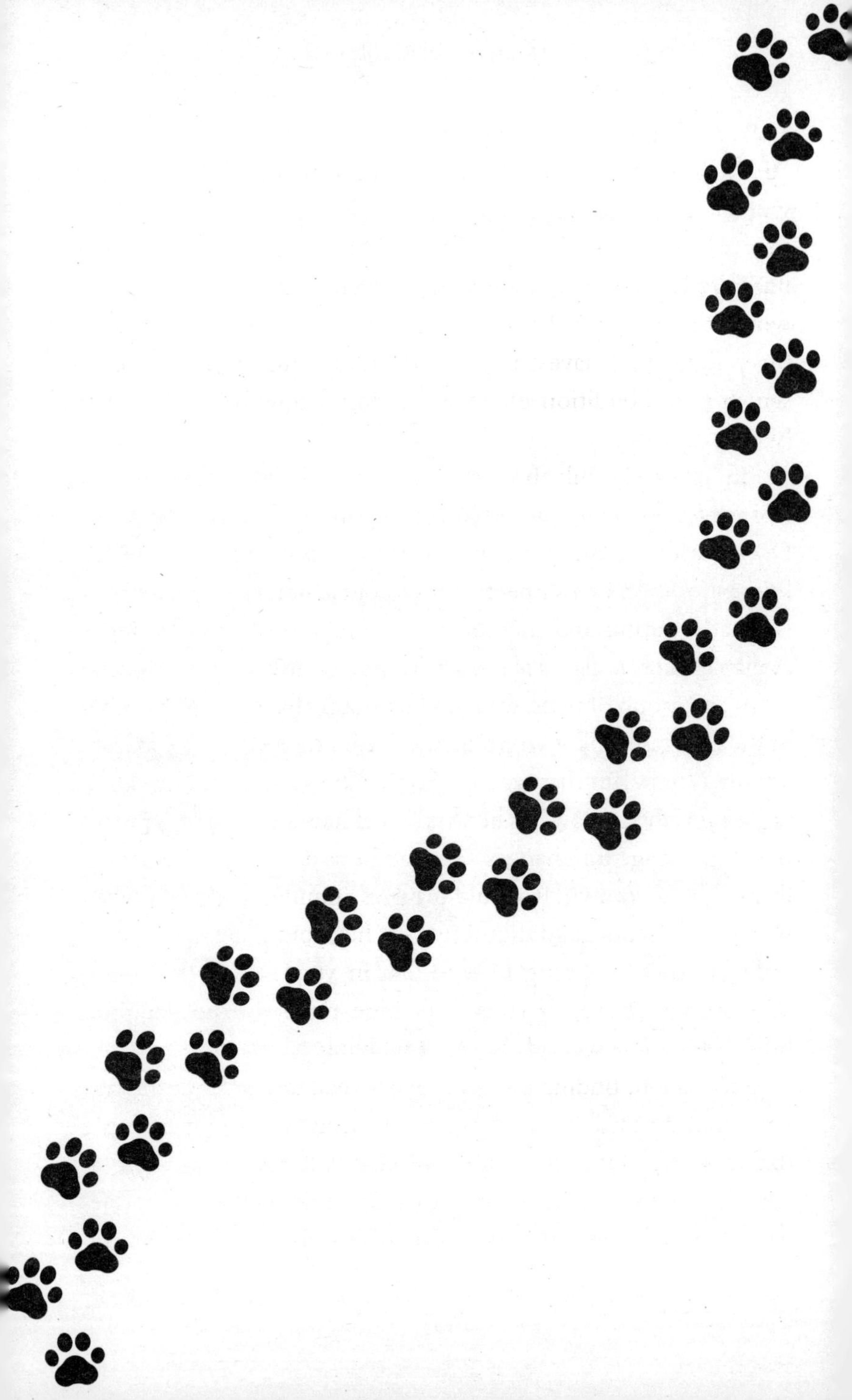

We all know the saying *barking up the wrong tree*. It originates from the practice of hunting squirrels and racoons. A dog will chase the squirrel or racoon until, like the cowards they are, they run up a tree, at which point the dog will helpfully and dutifully bark, their paws up on the tree to show their humans where the long-tailed poltroon is. Now, from time to time, the furry fiend will have subsequently leapt into another tree, at which point, tradition dictates, the dog is now barking up the 'wrong' tree.

But let's just think about this for a second. Do we criticise the FBI for following up the last known sighting of a missing person? Do we critique the murder detective who investigates the last known location of a suspect? No, of course not. Because we realise that a dutiful and methodical examination of the evidence available to us *at that time* is essential in any investigative process.

In any group of trees, we could randomly bark up any number of them in case, unknown to us, the craven moron above has leapt unseen into it. But that would be a thankless task and the odds of us being right are low. Yes, it would feel like we are being proactive. But change for changes' sake can be as dangerous as a default fear of the unknown. It would leave us running, frantically, from tree to tree, leaping and shouting 'Hey, hey, come down, you furry little moron, I'm going to bite you in your stupid fluffy tail.' While, high above, there is only high-pitched cruel laughter broken for a few seconds by quiet nibbling.

Life is about finding the balance between staying with the tree you're currently barking up and knowing when to bark up a different one. But here's something that will blow your mind. If we can't see the squirrel up in the canopy anyway then what does 'right tree' even mean? If you really think about it, there are no 'wrong' trees. Stretching in front of you, there's an entire forest of the right trees, just waiting for you to bark up them.

Here is an example from my own life. There are some who might have objected to the idea of a competition called Britain's Ugliest Pet. After all, it's a pretty strange thing to call a talent competition. It might have seemed like a very wrong tree indeed. But I knew that it was a chance to see the world beyond my front door. And if I had any doubts, they were soothed by Holly and Luke, who always told me that everyone was about to fall in love with me like they had. I was determined to just be myself.

But even I was surprised by the intensity of the reaction when I ended up winning the whole thing! Those days are lost in a blur of camera flashes and interviews as everyone seemed to want a piece of me. I remember there were a lot of sofas. I don't get the chance to watch much breakfast television usually — far too early in the day for a dog who likes her beauty sleep — but I was definitely surprised by how sofa-based it is.

From Yorkshire to London and TV fame — I thought I'd finally found my destiny. Here was 'my' tree. But little did I know the fickle squirrel of stardom had already jumped to the tree next door.

And, finally, it all came to a head when Holly and Luke received a mysterious call about a meeting that was to change my life.

Hollywood called.

Lesson 19: New tricks

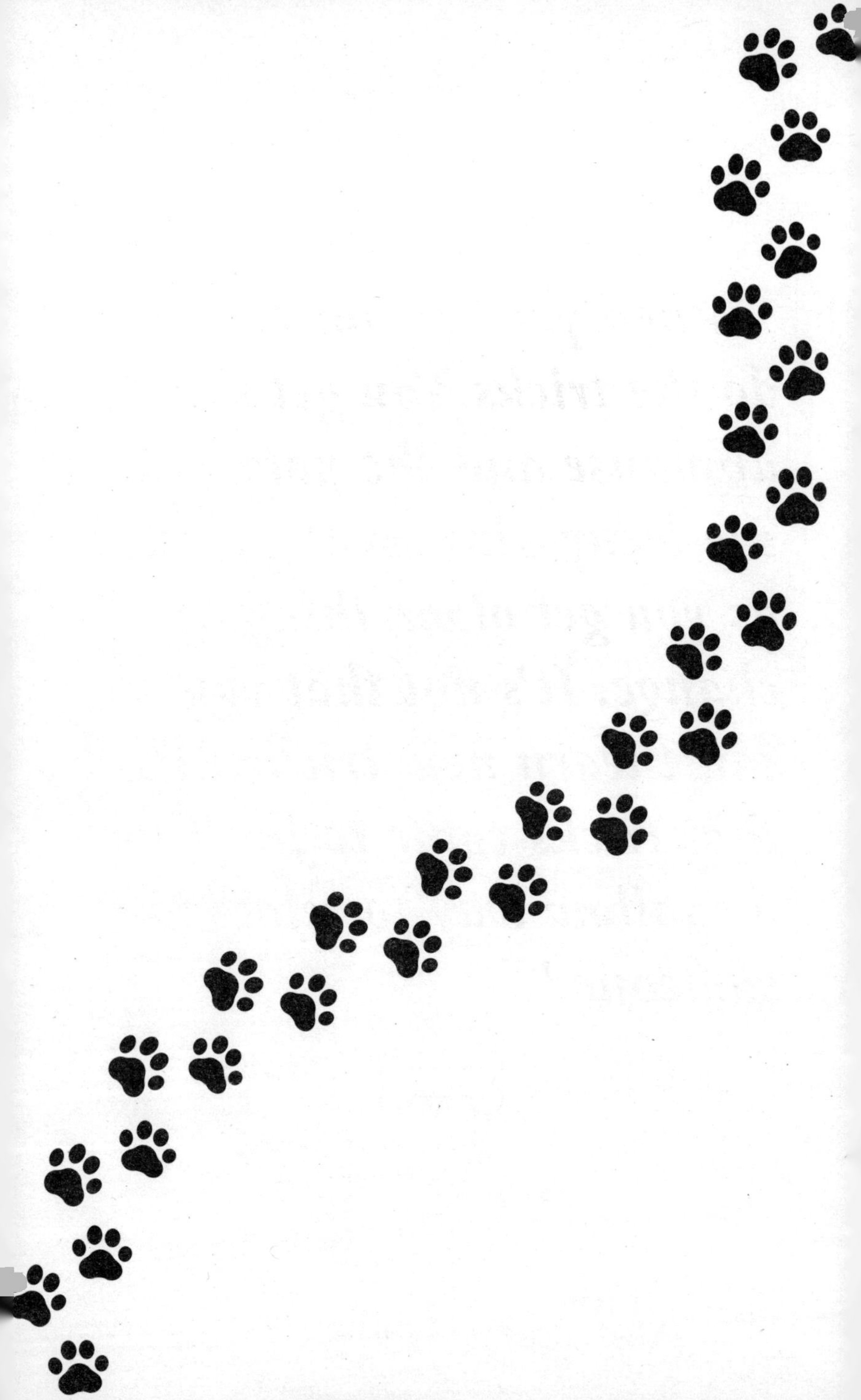

'When you're young, you do the tricks. You get the applause and the pats and the teeny-tiny treats. But, as you get older, things change. It's not that you can't learn new tricks. It's that tricks come to feel like a shallow way to relate to someone.'

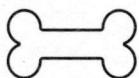

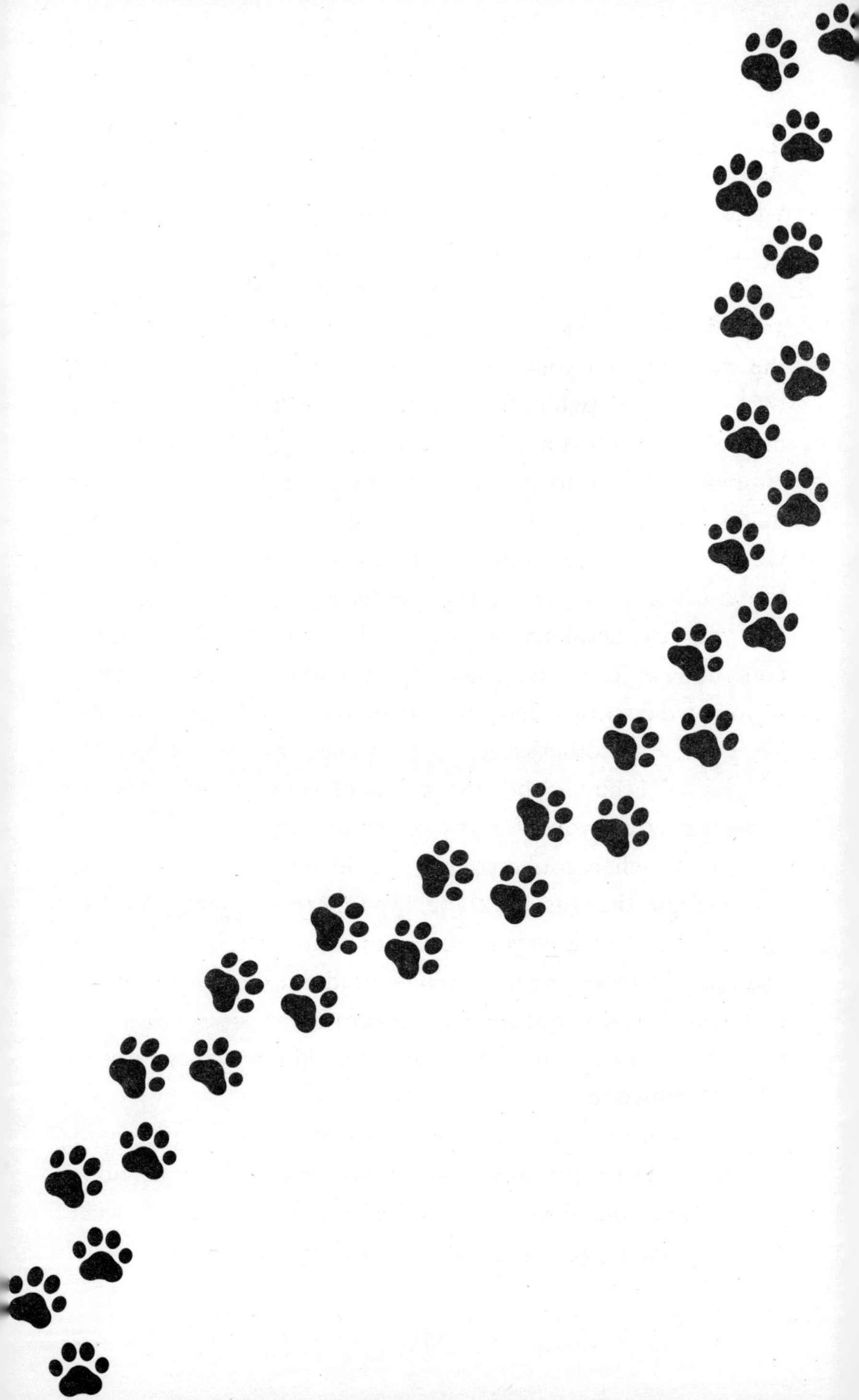

B efore we start, I'm aware of the famous saying about dogs of a certain age not being good acquirers of new skillsets. And while I certainly don't consider myself 'old' in any way. In my opinion you're only as old as the llama toy you snuggle with.

Basically, I think we've got this whole thing the wrong way around. When you're a puppy, unsure of yourself, you latch onto the tricks of your youth because they get a reaction. Stay. Roll over. Play dead (which we really need to have a word about because it is really not OK). The sitting thing, I admit I've never entirely been able to get my head around it. I don't mind a sit down. I've been known to do it from time to time. But, people, we have four legs. Standing is twice as comfortable for us as it is for you. And if we want to take the load off, there's lying down. But you guys absolutely LOVE it when we sit. The treats, the compliments. You can't enter a park without seeing a puppy surrounded by people entreating them to sit. Frankly it's awkward. We catch each other's eye, raise an eyebrow like, 'What you gonna do?' I think it's because you spend your lives sitting down. I've got news for you. It's really not good for *you*.

Anyway, when you're young, you do the tricks. You get the applause and the pats and the teeny-tiny treats. But, as you get older, things change. As you come into your doghood, you realise that life isn't about pretending to be dead in exchange for attention, you learn that you are enough already. It's not that you *can't* learn them. It's that suddenly tricks feel like a shallow way to relate to someone.

That's not to say I'm not a great believer in lifelong learning. When we learn new things, our brains form new connections. Our memory improves, as well as lowering stress and improving our confidence. We renew ourselves and our relationships with everyone around us. I had to practise this during the almost seven months I spent training before my movie debut. There was so much to get my head around. How to hit my mark, how to face the right way. We broke down my walk and built up a whole new one. We worked out how to make me lick A-listers' faces by adding an elegant dab of pate behind the ears.

Of course, there were parts of my training I've not had chance to show off onscreen yet. I'm still waiting for the call from *Dancing on Ice* or *American Idol*, but I'm a patient dog. No actor's training ever goes to waste. One day the world will need a Pug who knows jujitsu or who can hit the high notes in the Queen of the Night aria.

Still, on the first day of filming, amid the hustle and bustle of the set, the trailers and the crew, the lights, the security, when the clapperboard came down and they called action, it was everything I'd imagined when I was a pup staring at the television all those years before. I didn't need to think about my training or my lines, I just had to embrace my destiny. For all pugkind.

Lesson 20: How not to chase your own tail

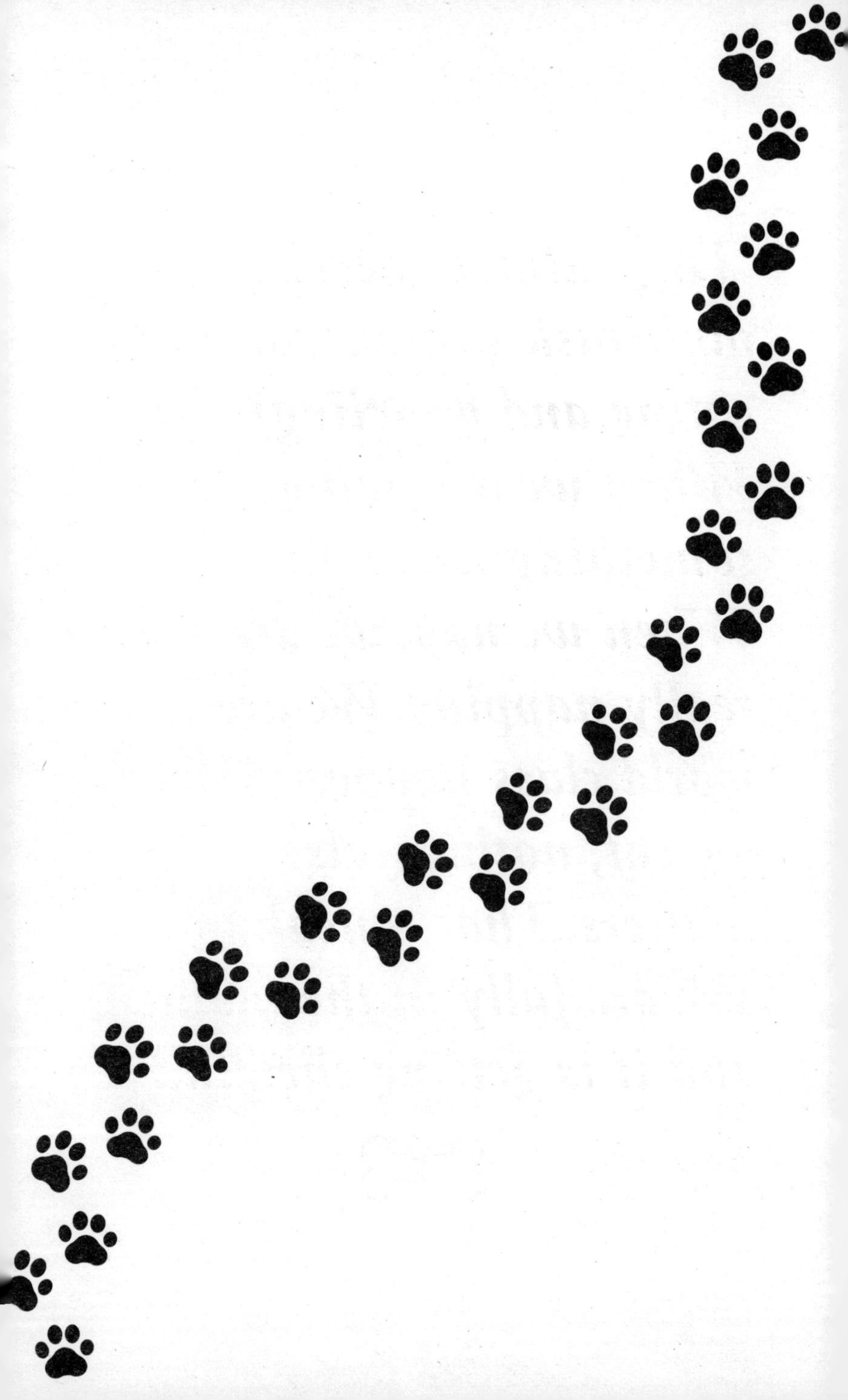

'Dogs almost never multitask (unless you count eating and growling). When we are doing something we're all in. When we nap, we are really napping. We are world class nappers. When we eat, nothing else matters. That squeaky toy? We are fully in the moment and it is getting chewed.'

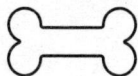

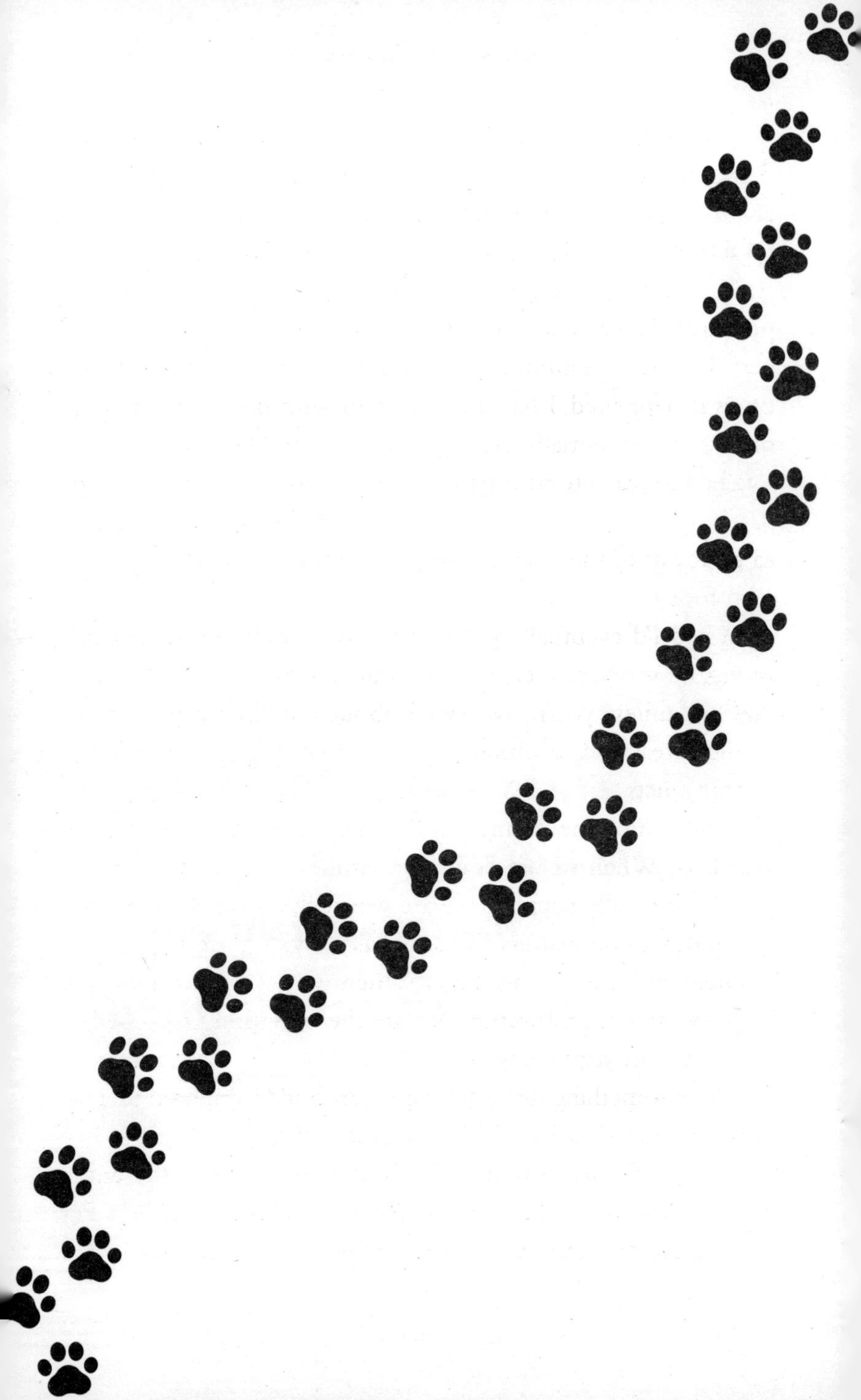

remember once, on set for a project, one of the stars was having trouble keeping their concentration in a scene. As with many creatives, he's a guy that likes to improvise. Like so many artists, he felt he just wasn't getting the line right. Take after take we tried, in different accents, moods and even using some interpretative dance. The problem was, the first take was still the best. He was questioning himself needlessly. After the first few times it happened, I had a quiet word with him and explained that he was essentially chasing his own tail. (This is something I've had to learn to deal with as I have a particularly distracting patch of hair on my tail, which is genuinely fascinating when I catch it out of the corner of my eye. I am also surprised by my own foot.)

When I'd eventually got him to concentrate on what I was saying, he was very receptive. You humans have a gift for worrying, but unless you're worrying about whether your dog has enough treats, I'd recommend you just keep it simple and trust your instincts.

Dogs almost never multitask (unless you count eating *and* growling). When we are doing something we're *all in*. When we nap, we are really napping. We are world class nappers. When we eat, nothing else matters. That squeaky toy? We are fully in the moment and it is getting *chewed*. When we get the zoomies, that is all we are doing. Tummy rubs are the only thing that matters while they are happening.

This is something that I think humans could learn from us. That focus on the task at hand. Take my *Deadpool* co-lead, Ryan. When it was time for us to film probably the key scene in the entire movie — the kiss — I made sure that it was all we focused on. For seven or eight minutes, we took take after take and I made sure that kiss was the centre of both of our universes. So much so that I'm not ashamed to admit I let out a few stinky little love-puffs.

When we had the shot, Ryan looked at me, eyes bright with tears, clearly overcome with emotion. 'Thank you,' he choked.

So, how do you focus on the job in hand and not your own tail, however charming it might be? I've got other tools in my arsenal, as well as the farting. Timeboxing is one of my favourite methods. This isn't anything to do with fighting, or time travel, instead it just means giving tasks the time they deserve then moving on.

For example:

- Trying to get a ball out from where it's got stuck under the sofa?
  I'd set aside a good two to three hours for something this vital.
- Worrying about what the Shitzu next door thinks of me?
  Less than a nanosecond.
- Sniffing a visitor's rump?
  Anything less than five minutes would be rude.
- Stressing about what to wear?
  Not worth the blink of an eye – if I even feel a wardrobe crisis coming on, I know it's easier to make it a naked but for a snazzy collar day (humans, I'm not suggesting you try this.)

Lesson 21: Make friends everywhere

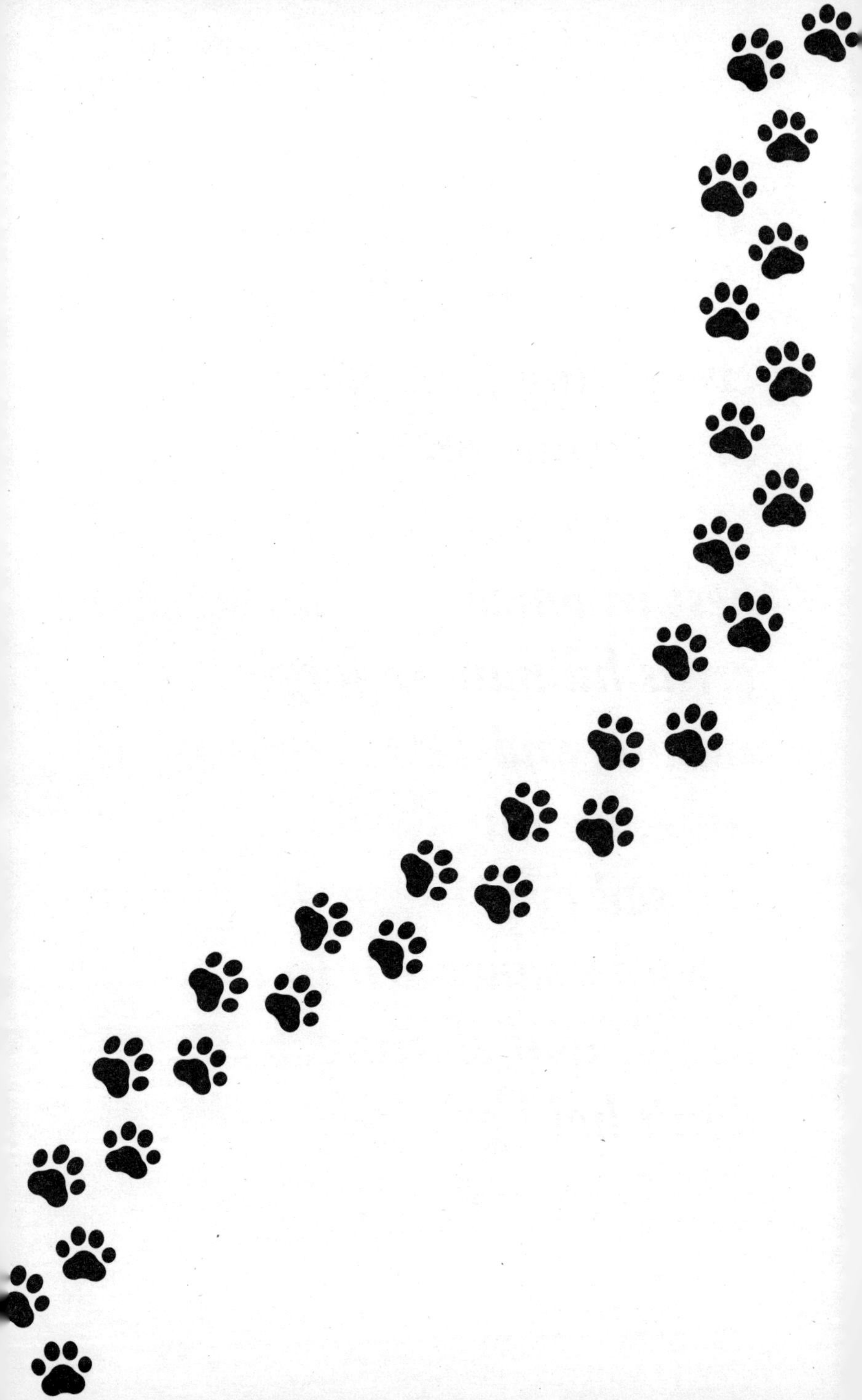

'Make no bones about it, we all need a friend sometimes. Our friends teach us everything from how to chase our dreams (or a ball), to tolerance and how to see the best in ourselves. They say to err is human, to forgive is canine, and I can see why. Sure, we might give you the old sad eyes if you dare to eat a bacon sandwich in front of us without sharing, but we don't hold grudges.'

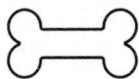

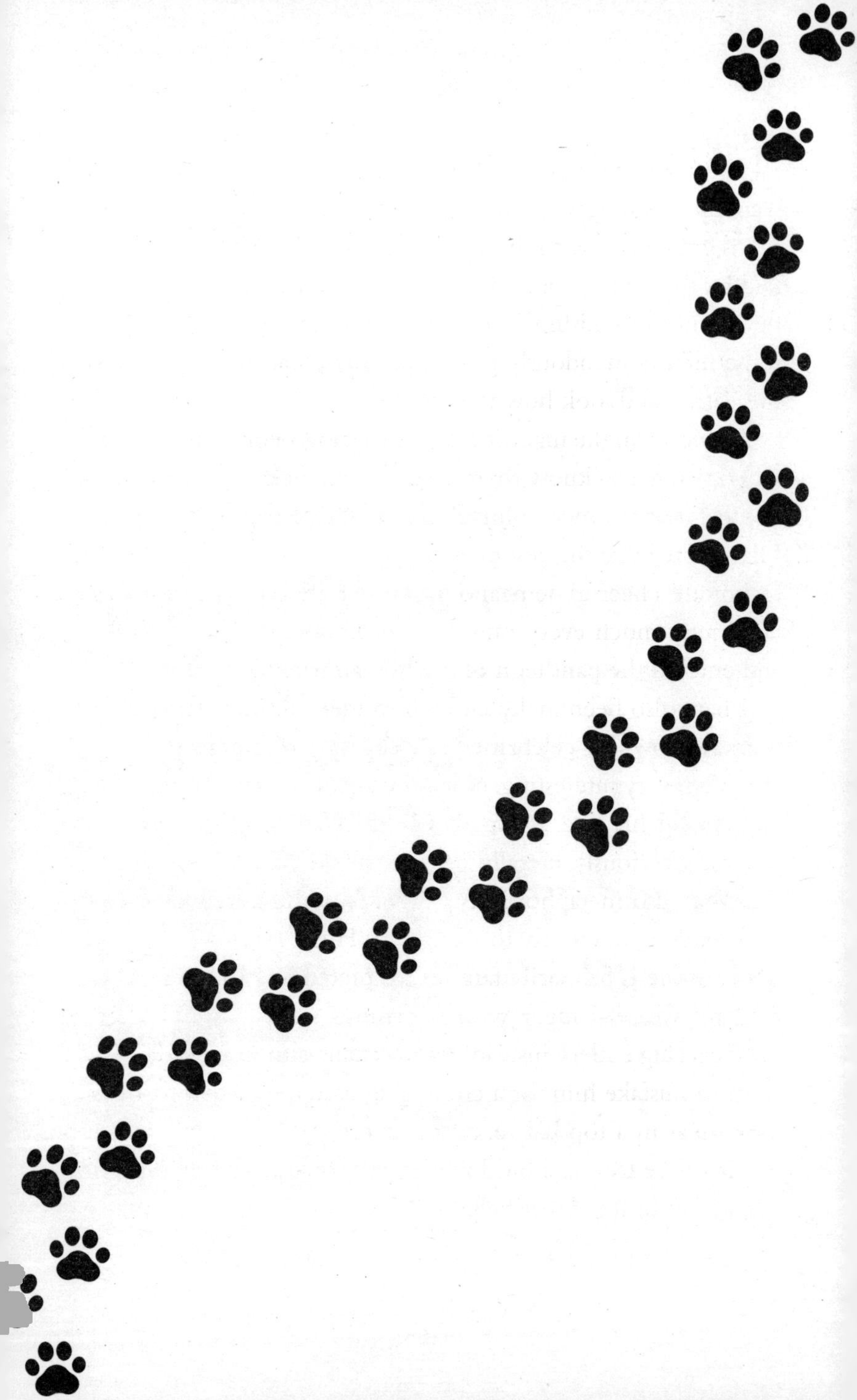

Y ou may have heard the phrase that strangers are just friends you haven't met yet. It isn't a hundred per cent accurate as sometimes strangers turn out to be pigeons, squirrels or enormous ginger cats with the cold dead eyes of a shark. It's also often said by the same people who say 'what is the only ship that will never sink? Friendship.' Then look you in the eye as if they've said something tremendously profound. Guys, that was the slogan for the *Titanic* and look how that worked out.

However, in the main, it is true that most people are wonderful when you get to know them. I have been lucky enough over the last few years to meet a huge variety of different sorts of people. I have to tell you the best ones are the children. Excellent stroking technique, cheerful demeanour, appropriate reverence for waggy tail. Pretty much every one of them has been an immediate hit and entered the pantheon of my human friends.

I have also been lucky enough to meet an interesting class of human known as 'celebrities'. Celebrities, or famous people, are also often very interesting. Not as interesting as children, but a still really solid hit rate. Ryan Reynolds is an absolute sweetie, as covered previously, literally because of the maple syrup immersions but also metaphorically as there's nothing he won't do for his friends. It was lovely to work with Hugh Jackman, who, as far as I'm aware is primarily famous for pretending to be some kind of giant weasel-badger with enormous sideburns and a set of meat carving cutlery instead of fingernails, although some people seem to mistake him for a circus ringmaster. Not that he doesn't look great in a top hat (extra tip: everyone looks great in a top hat. If you're feeling a bit down or overlooked, I'd suggest trying a huge hat to see if that helps).

Simon Pegg and Nick Frost were delightful and I believe are something to do with ice creams. Catherine Tate is charm personified and for the record, seemed unbothered when I accidentally sneezed on her. I was expecting Jimmy Carr to be a chauffeur, but instead he's actually really good at sitting behind a desk and laughing loudly.

Andy Serkis crawled around on all fours calling things 'his precious', which of course I could really relate to. After all, you people talk a lot about needing to be 'grounded' – you could start by using all four limbs a bit more rather than teetering about on your back legs all the time.

There's been so many more, too many to name. And it's been heartwarming beyond words how each one of them has welcomed me into their world. I've learnt so much from the stars who've shared their shows and dressing rooms with me. And as this book shows, I hope they've learnt something in return, especially if that thing is how we don't have to belong in just one little box. Bald, wrinkly or sporting a luxuriant mohawk? You don't have to pick one, you can have all three.

But if anything, these steps into the spotlight and the celebrity world have made me realise just how special the people who don't live in its glare are. As I travel the world now, I have made it my mission to give my utter focus to every single person I meet. Everyone deserves to feel like they are the most important person in the universe and I have made that my life goal. It doesn't matter if it's on a Manhattan street, or a remote Scottish island, I don't care how 'famous' you are.

Whether that means always pausing to receive a butt scratch, licking their face, or sitting down and lifting my knee so they can regard my nipples with awe.

The main thing I've learned is that happiness comes from being yourself. When you do that, you open up a space for everyone else to be themselves too. They start to smile, they sense that they can relax. And then the tummy rubs may begin.

That's how friendships start. Not just with tummy rubs – but by being yourself. And while people come and go, friends are the ones that stick around. I get it, life is hectic – I'm not always on the same continent or in the same time zone as my friends. But when we meet up to the chew the fat (and yes, I do mean that literally – gristle is life) – it's like we've never been apart.

Make no bones about it, we all need a friend sometimes. Our friends teach us everything from how to chase our dreams (or a ball), to tolerance and how to see the best in ourselves. They say to err is human, to forgive is canine, and I can see why. Sure, we might give you the old sad eyes if you dare to eat a bacon sandwich in front of us without sharing, but we don't hold grudges. So naturally, my top tip here is to get a friend who's a dog.

Your friends are the ones who'll pick you up when you're down, share their treats, jump in the mud with you and not mind if you occasionally let out a delicate little toot. They're also the ones who'll be honest with you if you do (dog forbid) start barking up the wrong tree (see earlier). They'll tell it to you straight if you get carried away or calm you down if you're worried a pigeon is giving you a funny look. They're the ones in your pack that help you be you.

In a world that too often celebrates sameness, I want to tell you to live your life without apology or fear of not conforming. Whatever your identity and background. If you've ever felt like an underdog, I want to tell you that you belong. You matter. Even the littlest of dogs can have a massive impact. Even if you have a scarily small tongue, an enormous excess of hair or unsettling micronipples. You deserve to be comfortable in your own skin (even if it's oddly smooth, wildly hairy or that rare perfect mix of wrinkly, tufty and glows in the light of the cameras).

You are enough. More than enough.

It doesn't matter wherever I've travelled to, Holly and Luke and I get home, we go for a walk in the woods, or on the beach and I am reminded what really matters in life. A short walk with the people you love most in the world, followed by a much longer carry and a large bowl of sausages.

Appendix A

FURTHER READING

As a look at this introductory reading list will show, dogs have long been at the centre of the literary world. I've included some personal favourites below:

The Hundred and One Dalmatians by Dodie Smith

The Adventures of Tintin by Hergé

Dog Man by Dav Pilkey

Max the Miracle Dog by Kerry Irving

Marley & Me by John Grogan

Tina: The Dog Who Changed the World by Niall Harbison

The Incredible Journey by Sheila Burnford

Sophie from Romania by Rory Cellan-Jones

Snoopy by Charles M Schulz

Meet Ella: The Dog Who Saved my Life by James Middleton

Greyfriars Bobby by Eleanor Stackhouse Atkinson

Marley & Me by John Grogan

A Dog's Purpose by W. Bruce Cameron

The Art of Racing in the Rain by Garth Stein

Lassie Come-Home by Eric Knight

The Curious Incident of the Dog in the Night-Time by Mark Haddon

Dog on It by Spencer Quinn

Travels with Charley: In Search of America by John Steinbeck.

Clifford the Big Red Dog by Norman Bridwell

The Plague Dogs by Richard Adams
Flush: A Biography by Virginia Woolf
Lad: A Dog by Albert Payson Terhune
The Red Dog by Louis de Bernières
If Cats Disappeared from the World by Genki Kawamura

Appendix B

I've got eclectic musical tastes — everything from Bach to Boney M — but these are my favourites and always make it onto my travel playlist:

- **'Hound Dog'** — Elvis Presley
- **'Howlin' for You'** — The Black Keys
- **'Hounds of Love'** — Kate Bush
- **'Black Dog'** — Led Zeppelin
- **'Old Dog'** — The Kinks
- **'Dog Eat Dog'** — Adam and the Ants
- **'I Wanna Be Your Dog'** — The Stooges
- **'Puppy Love'** — Donny Osmond
- **'The Dogs of War'** — Pink Floyd
- **'Atomic Dog'** — George Clinton / Parliament—Funkadelic)
- **'Diamond Dogs'** — David Bowie
- **'Sick As A Dog'** — Aerosmith
- **'Walking the Dog'** — Rufus Thomas, covered by The Rolling Stones
- **'Hair of the Dog'** — Nazareth
- **'Who Let the Dogs Out?'** — Baha Men
- **'Dogs of Lust'** — The The
- **'Man's Best Friend (Dog)'** — George Clinton
- **'Bitch'** — Meredith Brooks
- **'I'm Just a Dog'** — Paul McCartney
- **'See A Dog'** — Chumbawamba

- **'The Puppy Song'** — Harry Nilsson
- **'Me and My Dog'** — John Denver

Beware:

- **'Dog Days Are Over'** — Florence + The Machine
- **'Year of the Cat'** — Al Stewart)
- **'What's New Pussycat?'** — Tom Jones
- **'Cool for Cats'** — Squeeze
- **'Cat's in the Cradle'** — Harry Chapin
- **'The Lovecats'** — The Cure

[Also anything by Pussycat Dolls or Atomic Kitten. Cat Stevens changed his name, so is acceptable.]

Appendix C

If you do need an occasional break from watching *Dogpool*, and yet still want to enjoy a good film not spoilt by too many cats or squirrels, here are some I can recommend:

- **Lassie** (1994)
- **The Call of the Wild** (2020)
- **Beethoven** (1992)
- **Lady and the Tramp** (1955)
- **K-9** (1989)
- **Turner & Hooch** (1989)
- **Best in Show** (2000)
- **White Fang** (1991)
- **Napoleon** (1985)
- **Dances with Wolves** (1990)
- **Homeward Bound: The Incredible Journey** (1993)
- **All Dogs go to Heaven** (1989)

NB: Don't try to tell me **Old Yeller** should be on this list. I don't need the trauma.

Acknowledgements

First off, a round of slobbery kisses to my mum and dad, Luke and Holly. Thanks for putting up with the snorts, snores, and fecal fiascoes in inappropriate places. You truly are my ride-or-dies (literally—you drive me everywhere).

To my older brothers, Max and Zak: thanks for the sneaky midnight cuddles and the contraband snacks slipped under the table. You know I'll never confess who my favorite is…unless there's bacon involved.

Big shoutout to my lawyer, Paul. Thanks for keeping me out of paw-sonal injury lawsuits and copyright infringements—apparently you can't just claim "the pug made me do it" as a defence. Who knew?

My agent, Lianne, and her globe-trotting sidekick, Super Gab—thank you for hauling me around the world, carrying my snacks, and tolerating my diva-level hotel demands (yes, I did ask for rose petals in the water bowl).

Glam-ma—thank you for keeping my brothers on a short leash whenever we travel. Without you, there'd be total mutt-ny.

To snack-feeder Frankie and the worlds best dog sitter, Aunty Jess: my stomach and I are eternally grateful. And Simon, thanks for not pressing charges after the Great Poppadom Incident of 2024. I regret nothing.

Maya—my comic convention sister from another mister, personal bodyguard (no touching, please), and fellow Swifty. I'll never forget the time I made a daring escape, and you went full action-hero, chasing me down and literally hurling yourself across the floor to stop me—knees grazed, pride dented, but mission accomplished. That's true love.

Dan the camera man—thanks for always filming me from my good side (which, let's face it, is all of my sides). You've turned my snorts, sneezes, and dramatic slow-motion snack dives into pure cinematic magic.

Gen, my publisher, you're the reason my wise (and wrinkly) words are reaching the masses. May your pen always be mightier than my chew toys.

Jamie—the wizard who turned my zoomies, side-eye stares and random pug wisdom into actual words on paper. Since it's tricky to type with paws (trust me, I've tried), thank you for being my human voice and making sure my genius could be shared with the world.

Ryan Reynolds—thank you for taking a chance on an unknown pup with zero acting credentials, questionable table manners, and an impressive ability to fart mid-scene.

And finally, to my fans across the globe: you are the kibble to my Kong, the squeak in my toy, and the warm spot on my favorite couch cushion. Without you, I'd just be another bald pup snoring on the sofa—but with you, I'm ~~Dogpool~~ the dog who played Dogpool (thanks, Paul).

Harper North

would like to thank the following staff and contributors for
their involvement in making this book a reality:

Sarah Burke
Alan Cracknell
Jonathan de Peyer
Anna Derkacz
Tom Dunstan
Kate Elton
Sarah Emsley
Simon Gerratt
Monica Green
Natassa Hadjinicolaou
Emma Hatlen
Jess Haycox
Taslima Khatun
Megan Jones
Rachel McCarron
Vincent Kelleher
Emily Thomas

Jo Ireson
Alice Murphy-Pyle
Genevieve Pegg
Laura Amos
Bobbie Slade
Eleanor Slater
Hilary Stein
Jess Haycox
Katrina Troy
Poppy McLoughlin
Claire Ward
Dean Russell
Amanda Percival
Lydia Grange
Hannah Williamson
Millie Morton
Matthew Richardson

For more unmissable reads,
sign up to the HarperNorth newsletter at
www.harpernorth.co.uk

or find us on socials at
@HarperNorthUK

**Harper
North**